Frederick James Furnivall

Hymns to the Virgin and Christ, the Parliament of Devils, and Other Religious Poems

Chiefly from the Archbishop of Canterbury's Lambeth MS. no.853

Frederick James Furnivall

Hymns to the Virgin and Christ, the Parliament of Devils, and Other Religious Poems
Chiefly from the Archbishop of Canterbury's Lambeth MS. no.853

ISBN/EAN: 9783337156060

Printed in Europe, USA, Canada, Australia, Japan

Cover: Foto ©Lupo / pixelio.de

More available books at **www.hansebooks.com**

Hymns to the Virgin & Christ,

The Parliament of Devils,

and other

Religious Poems,

CHIEFLY FROM

THE ARCHBISHOP OF CANTERBURY'S LAMBETH MS. No. 853.

EDITED BY

FREDERICK J. FURNIVALL,

M.A., TRIN. HALL, CAMB.; MEMBER OF COUNCIL OF THE PHILOLOGICAL
AND EARLY ENGLISH TEXT SOCIETIES.

———————

LONDON:

PUBLISHED FOR THE EARLY ENGLISH TEXT SOCIETY,
BY N. TRÜBNER & CO., 60, PATERNOSTER ROW.

MDCCCLXVII.

PREFACE.

AFTER telling Mrs Gaskell one day a story for the truth of which I could not vouch, she said, with her beautiful bright smile, " Now I'm going to believe that, whether it's true or not. It ought to be true." On looking through the Lambeth MS. 853, which Mr Stubbs kindly handed to me in Lambeth Palace Library, I could not help saying, " I'll print it all, whether it contains early versions or late ; it *is* a jolly little Manuscript " :—a chubby vellum quarto, written in a large, clear, upright hand, which looked at first sight fourteenth century, but which the Museum authorities whom I afterwards consulted put at about 1430 A.D. As nice a little volume as one would wish to handle ; a pleasing contrast to the shabby, scrubby, paper Percy folio of two hundred years later that I am now working at. Accordingly, the whole MS. is in type for the Society, and I hope members have no cause to regret it, for though earlier versions of some of the poems are no doubt in existence,—I have printed one at least sixty years older at pp. 106, 108, 110, 112, to show how the late text has changed [1]—yet the Lambeth MS. has given us the better text of *The Complaint of Christ*, in " Political, Religious, and Love Poems," (E.E.T.S., 1866,) a better text of " The Parliament of Devils " than that printed by Wynkyn de Worde, and the best texts yet printed of the far-famed *Stans Puer ad Mensam*, " How the Good Wife taught her Daughter," and " How the Wise Man taught his Son," &c.: these, besides other poems of considerable

[1] Two words at least of the earlier text—*sauʒten* and *vnsauʒte*, " to reconcile " and " unreconciled, at enmity," p. 108, l. 37-38, were unknown to the late scribe, and were changed by him to *soften* and *unsoft*.

beauty and interest in the present volume, and the other Texts I
have lately edited, or am now editing, for the Society.   The early
Englishman, like the modern one, was a religious and superstitious
person, and as any one in 2360 A.D. should know of us, that in many
educated (or deducated[1]) persons' minds now, baptism by an epis-
copally-ordained clergyman is necessary to salvation, that a man's
being drowned while boating on Sunday is a just judgment of God,
whereas a similar death on Monday is a sad accident, with a hundred
other like notions[2]; so we should know of our forefathers, if we would
estimate them aright, what their religious belief and superstitious
fancies were. Mary-worship, Parliament of Devils, Stations of Rome,
St Gregory's Trental, and what not : let us have them all : all the non-
sense, as well as the expressions of the pure, simple faith, that through
life and death our men of old held to.   And a survey of our early
religious poetry will, I believe,—and so far as I may speak from some
work at it,—result in a verdict favourable to the plain good sense

---

[1] We sadly want some word like this *deducate, deducation,* &c., to denote the
wilful down-leading into prejudice and unreason, in Politics at least, so prevalent in
England and everywhere else, to support unjust social arrangements and abuses
because they exist, or are in the interest of a powerful class, &c. Let any one think
of the amount of deducation attempted about the Repeal of the Corn Laws, the old
and modern Reform Bills, the late American War, &c., and then see how hard the
deducators still are at their work !

[2] " Dr Pusey has written another letter to the *Times,* stating his opinion of
absolution. He believes that Christ, conferring upon the Apostles the power to
remit sins, intended to confer it also upon their ' successors ' He therefore holds
that every successor has the power to remit the sins of penitent persons as fully as
Christ himself could have done ; and so he affirms, on the authority of the Ordination
Service, the Church of England also holds. *In other words,* Christ intended to
leave the salvation of souls dependent on the will of such human beings as can be
proved to have been ordained by the ordained up through the ages to Himself. One
single unordained Bishop, say in the middle ages or the third century, would spoil
the whole arrangement. Why does not Dr Pusey claim the power of working
miracles given to the Apostles at the same time ? The invisibility of the power is
no greater obstacle in the one case than the other. If the sick did not get visibly
better for the priest's touch, neither do the bad get visibly better for his absolution.
After all, does the human race advance ? A Roman gentleman would have smiled
at a superstition so gross as that which Dr Pusey dignifies with the name of
Christianity." 1866, Dec. 1, *The Spectator,* p. 1326, col. 1-2. Dr Pusey and his
school may not admit the correctness of the statement above, " In other words."
I only wish to register here the opinion of one of our best edited weeklies on this
point, and to note that however comical the view stated, and a thousand like ones,
may seem to our man of 2360 A.D. they were equally so to many in 1866 A.D.

and practical going straight at the main point which Englishmen
pride themselves on, whatever amount of philistinism and humbug
is mixed up with these qualities. The burden of the early songs (as
I read them) is a prayer for forgiveness of sins, a desire to get out of
the filth of the flesh, and rise, as well here as hereafter, into the
purer and higher life which, to the believer, union with his
Saviour implied and implies.

Many of the poems in this volume seem to me very touching and
beautiful, and I hope other readers will find them so too. The most
interesting to me is the one I have entitled, from l. 638 in it, p. 78,
"The Mirror of the Periods of Man's Life, or Bids of the Virtues
and Vices for the Soul of Man," pp. 58-78. It sketches the tempt-
ations of the well-off man of the period—the MS. is ab. 1430 A.D.
—from the time when he was new-born from his mother till, at a
hundred years old, Overhope and Wanhope (despair) would ruin him,
but Good Hope and Good Faith bring him to trust in God's mercy. At
twenty—which may be a misprint for fifteen, xx for xv,—this is the
choice presented to the young man.

> Quod resoun, " in age of .xx. 3eer.
>   Goo to oxenford, or lerne lawe."
> Quod lust, " harpe & giterne þere may y leere,
>   And pickid staffe & buckelere, þere-wiþ to plaue,
> At tauerne to make wommen myrie cheere,
>   And wilde felawis to-gidere drawe,
> And be to bemond ¹ A good squyer
>   Al ny3t til þe day do dawe.

¹ For an explanation of this *bemond*, I have asked in vain Mr Chappell, Mr
Way, Mr Morris, Mr Skeat, Mr Wright, &c., &c. The only interpretation I can
suggest is drawn from a passage in Le Venery de Twety, Cotton MS. Vesp. B. xii.,
printed in *Reliquiæ Antiquæ*, vol. I., pp. 149-154. At pp. 152-3 we read, of the
hounds hunting the hare, " And if eny fynde of hym, where he hath ben, Rycher or
Bemond, ye shall say, *oyez a* Bemond *le vayllaunt, que quide trovere le coward, ou le
court cow.*" The name *Bemond* might easily pass from the leading hound to the
leader of a revel, or be used, by personification, for a fancied god of indulgence in
women and wine, a sort of Bacchus. I think it certain that this *bemond* has nothing
to do with the *bemol* (flat, ♭), and *bequarre* (natural, the square b, ♮) of the curious
song on learning music in *Reliquiæ Antiquæ*, vol. I., p. 292, or the *bemy* of the
Burlesque, p. 83, *ib.* last line. In our early music books B is *si*, though in the
earliest I have seen, no name is given to it.

Conscience's remonstrance that this will waste his friends' money and his own time and learning, is answered by

"Good conscience, goo preche to þe post,
þi councel saueriþ not my tast . . .
Al my lust y wole ful-fille,
I wole spare no womman."

After the advice of Pride, Gluttony, Lechery, Wrath, Envy, Sloth, Covetousness, and Avarice, to the young man, how to indulge his passions and lusts, comes Pride again with this bit of counsel as to dress :

"Apparaile þe propirli," quod Pride,
"Loke þi pockettis passe þe lengist gise ;
Slatre þi clothis boþe schorte & side [= wide]
Passinge all oþere mennis sise."

And so the poem continues with allusions, more or less, to the manners of the times. The *pockettis* of the verses last quoted serve to fix the date of the composition of the poem, if they are (as I suppose them to be) what Camden in his *Remaines*, p. 196, calls "*pocketting sleeves*." [1] He says

"Of the long pocketting sleeves in the time of King Henry the Fourth, Hocclive, a master of that age, sings,

Now hath this land little need of broomes
To sweep away the filth out of the streete,
Sen side sleeves of pennilesse groomes
Will it up licke, be it dry or weete."

The woodcut of the Duke of Gloucester[?] on p. 153 of Mr Fairholt's *Costume in England*, copied from the Royal MS. 15 E 4 (fol. 14), in the British Museum, shows the long pocket sleeve admirably, and 'his crimson jacket furred with deep red is exceedingly short,' but gathered in close folds behind. At p. 159 of Fairholt is another woodcut of an attendant with the pocket sleeve, from the same Royal MS. 14 E 4. On fol. 133 of the same Royal MS. are three figures with the long pocket sleeves, and one of them has his sleeves tied

---

[1] Pockets begin to appear in women's dresses in Edward the Third's time, says Fairholt, and are shown in that king's daughter's dress on the south side of his tomb in Westminster Abbey, as copied in Fairholt, p. 100.

behind his back, just below the bottom of his jacket. The very
wide and short doublet seems not to have appeared till about
1460, and not to have been slashed. The tighter plaited jacket
of Edward the Fourth's reign, also contemporary with pocket sleeves,
had "large sleeves, open at the sides to display the shirt beneath," as
shown in the cut on pages 154 and 159 of Fairholt. This is the only
slatring (supposing it means *slashing*) shown in the figures, unless the
opening for the arm in the long pocket sleeve be meant by the words
of the poem. But the slashing of garments was at least as early as
Chaucer's 'so mochil pounsyng of chiseles to make holes, so moche
daggyng of sheris' (*Persones Tale*, ed. Wright, p. 143, col. 2).

The *rere* or late suppers noticed in l. 374 of this Mirror poem are
complained of by Roberd of Brunne in 1303. *Handlyng Synne*, p.
226, l. 7260-3. (See also the servants' 'rere sopers' denounced, l.
7268-79.)

> Rere sopers yn pryuyte,
>
> Wyþ glotonye echone þey be ;
>
> And þyr is moche waste ynne,
>
> And gadryng of ouþer synne.

Doubtless Roberd was not the first preacher who inveighed against
them. He also complains of the rich man lying long in bed on
Sundays.

> When he heryþ a bel ryng
>
> To holy cherche men kallyng,
>
> þan may he not hys bedde lete,
>
> But þan behoueþ hym lygge and swete,
>
> And take þe mery mornyng slepe.

Handlyng Synne, p. 135, l. 4258-62.

For the last three Poems in this volume I am indebted to Mr W.
Aldis Wright, who copied them from MSS. under his charge in the
Library of the Trinity College, Cambridge. The first, *Quindecim
Signa ante diem Judicii*, he desired to print on account of its
variations from the other earlier versions of the Poem in the E.E.
Poems I edited for the Philological Society (Transactions 1858, Pt.
II. pp. 7-12), in Hampole's Pricke of Conscience, the Metrical Homilies
edited by Mr Small (in E. E. Poems as above, pp. 162-3), &c. The

second forms a companion to the Virgin's Complaint in our *Political,
Religious, and Love Poems*, 1866, and the third is given for its
historic interest, and its contrast to the temper in which the later
chronicler wrote of Archbishop Scrope's death.

Some of the poems bear traces of having been Southernized from
a Northern original, as in using *boon* for *bane*, p. 25, l. 108, *las-
tande na mare*, l. 115, *siʒhande*, p. 30, l. 261, and Mr Perry has just
sent me a version from the Northern Thornton MS. of the Sweetness of
Jesus, pp. 8-11, here, pp. 83-6 of the Text edited by Mr Perry from
the Thornton MS. that will appear with this one. I have only in con-
clusion to return thanks to the Archbishop of Canterbury for the
loan of his pretty little Manuscript, and to Mr Aldis Wright for his
help, always so willingly given, notwithstanding the pressure of
crowds of other work that would overwhelm an ordinary man.

3 St George's Square, N.W.
    12th November, 1866.

CORRIGENDA.

P. 27, l. 171. *Lijknes* is no doubt a miswriting of the MS. for *sijknes*,
sickness.

P. 61, l. 96. *Put* ″ *after* dawe.

P. 119, l. 38. *For* dryve. *read* dryve, (comma for full stop).

CONTENTS.

		Page
Contents of the Lambeth MS. 853	. . .	xv-xvi
Notes	. . . .	xvii-xviii

HYMNS TO THE VIRGIN.

Veni, Coronaberis	.	1-3
(A Song of great Sweetness from Christ to his daintiest Dam)		
Hail, Blessed Mary !		4-5
Aue Maria	.	6-7

POEMS TO CHRIST.

The Sweetness of Jesus	.	8-11
Be my Coumfort, Crist Ihesus ! . . .	.	12-14
Richard de Castre's Prayer to Jesus . .	.	15-17
Do Merci bifore thi Iugement . . .	.	18-21
The Love of Jesus	.	22-31
Se what oure Lord suffride for oure Sake . .	.	32-4
I wiyte my silf myn owne Woo . .	.	35-9
The Virtues of the Name Jesus (in Prose) . .	.	40

OTHER RELIGIOUS POEMS.

The Deuelis Perlament, or Parlamentum of Feendis	.	41-57
The Mirror of the Periods of Man's Life . .		58-78
(Or Bids of the Virtues & Vices for the Soul of Man)		
God send us Paciens in oure Olde Age . .		79-82
This World is but a Vanyte (An Old Man's Lament)	.	83-5
This World is false and vain . . .	.	86-7

c

		Page
Earth		88-90
Reuertere (In Englisch Tunge "Turne Aȝen ! ") . . .		91-4
Merci passith Riȝtwisnes		95-100
(A Dialogue between a despairing Sinner and Mercy)		
The Belief		101-3
The Ten Commandments		104-5

Keep Wel Cristes Comaundement : two texts,

I. from the Vernon MS. (Bodleian Libr.) ab. 1370 A.D.; even pages 106-112
II. from the Lambeth MS. 853 ab. 1430 A.D.; odd pages . 107-113

The Sixtene Poyntis of Charite . . .		. 114-117
Quindecim Signa ante diem Judicij . . .		118-25
Who can not wepe, com lerne of me . .		. 126-7
(The Virgin's Lament over her dead Son)		
The Death of Archbishop Scrope (8 June, 1405) .		128
Extract from Halle's *Vnion* as to Archbp. Scrope's Death .		129-30
Glossary		131-137
Notes		137
Index of First Lines		138-9

CONTENTS OF THE LAMBETH MS. 853.

Page of MS.

1. Surge mea Sponsa . 1
   (printed here p. 1-3.)

2. In a Tabernacle. *Quia
   Amore langueo.* . 4
   (Political, Religious, and Love Poems,
   E. E. T. Soc., 1866, p. 148-50.)

3. In a valey . . . 7
   (Pol., Rel., & L. Poems, 1866, p. 150-8.)

4. Ihesu þi swetnes . 14
   (printed here p. 8-11.)

5. Ihesus þat sprong . 20
   (here p. 12-14.)

6. Heil be þou Marie . 24
   (here p. 4-5.)

7. Heil be þou Marie . 26
   (here p. 6-7.)

8. Oratio R. de Castre . 28
   (here p. 15-17.)

9. Whoso wilneþ . ⎫
   Aristotle's A B C. ⎬ 30
   (Babees Boke, &c., E. E. T. Soc.,
   1867, p. 11-12.)

10. Whi is þis world biloued 32
    (here p. 86-7.)

11. Erþe out of erþe . . 35
    (here p. 88-90.)

12. In þee, god fadir . ⎫
    The Belief. ⎬ 39
    (here p. 101-3.)

13. Man among þi myrþis. ⎫
    The 16 points of ⎬ 42
    Charity ⎭
    (here p. 114-7.)

14. Every man schulde ⎫
    teche þis lore or ⎪
    The Ten Command- ⎬ 47
    ments ⎪
    (here p. 104-5.) ⎭

15. I warne eche liif or ⎫
    The Ten Command- ⎬ 49
    ments (here p. 107-113.) ⎭

16. There is no creature ⎫
    Do mercy bifore þi ⎬ 54
    iugement ⎪
    (here p. 18-21.) ⎭

17. As y gan wandre or ⎫
    This world is but a ⎬ 58
    vanyte . ⎪
    (here p. 83-5.) ⎭

18. In a noon tijd . ⎫
    Reuertere (here p. 91-4.) ⎬ 61

19. Bi a forest . ⎫
    Right wole forþ . ⎬ 66
    (here p. 95-100.)

20. As resoun rewlid or ⎫
    Filius Regis . ⎬ 74
    (Polit., Religious, and Love Poems,
    E. E. T. Soc., 1866, p. 205-13.)

21. This is goddis owne
    complaint . . 81
    (Political, Religious, and Love
    Poems, 1866, p. 161-9.)

21. If þou wole be well . 88
    (Prose. Here p. 40.)

21. Loue is lijf (here p. 22-31.) 90

Page
of MS.

22. The good wijf tauȝte hir
douȝtir . . . 102
(Babees Boke, &c., E. E. T. Soc.,
1867, p. 36-47.)

23. From þe tyme . } 113
Goil send us paciens }
(here p. 79-82.)

24. Bothe ȝonge & olde . 117
(here p. 32-4.)

25. How Mankinde dooþ }
bigynne . } 120
The Mirror . }
(here p. 58-78.)

26. Mi dere sone . } 150
Stans Puer . }
(Babees Boke, &c., E. E. T. Soc.,
1867, p. 27-33.)

27. Sone y schal þee }
schewe . }
Se what Our Lord } 155
suffride (here p. 32-4) }

Page
of MS.

28. Whanne Mary was }
greet . . } 157
Parliament of Devils }
(here p. 41-57.)

29. If so be þat lechis . 182
(Babees Boke, &c., E. E. T. Soc.,
1867, p. 54-8.)

30. Listniþ lordingis }
How the wise man } 186
taught his Son }
(Babees Boke, &c., p. 48-52.)

31. Thus oure gracious god }
The Complaint of } 193
Christ . }
(Political, Rel., and Love Poems,
1866, p. 169-203.)

32. In my ȝonge age } 226
I wiyte my silf myn } to
owne woo . } 233
(here p. 35-9.)

NOTES.

Pref. p. iv, l. 7. A just judgment of God. Compare Cotgrave's "*Vue lambe de dieu*. Soe doe the canting and blasphemous rogues of France tearme a cankered, gangrened, or desperately-sore leg. A.D. 1611.

p. 35. *I wiyte myself myn owne woo*. Sir F. Madden, in his Introduction to *Syr Gawayne*, p. lxv, notes another copy of this, "a Poem in ten eight-line stanzas, the burden of which is 'I wite my self myne owne wo,' on fol. 71 of MS. Rawlinson, C. 86, Bodleian Library. It begins 'In my youthe fulle wylde I was.'" Another is printed from MS. Cotton. Calig. A ii fol. 106, v° in *Reliquiæ Antiquæ*, v. 1, p. 197-200. It is in 15 stanzas of 8, with two introductory lines :

> I may say, and so may mo,
> I wyte mysylfe myue owene woo.

p. 41. "The *Parlyament of Deuylles*" was also "Enprynted In London In Powels chyrcheyarde By Julyan Notary. A. M. M.CCCCC. & xx "; and Wynkyn de Worde's edition of 1509 was "reprinted by Nicol for R. Heber, Esq., as his contribution to the Roxburghe Club, but for private reasons, never issued to its members." *Bohn's Lowndes*. Colophon. "Thus endeth the parlyament of deuylles. Enprynted by Wynkyn de word / prynter unto the moost excellent pryncesse my lady the kynges moder. The yere of our lorde .M.CCCCC. & ix."

p. 58. *The Mirror*. In Admiral Swinburne's incomplete copy of *The noble lyfe & natures of man Of bestes / serpentys / fowles & fisshes y' be moste knowen*, by Laure*n*s A*n*drewe of y₀ towne of Calis, is a large cut running across both pages (a iii b, a iv), of the Ten Ages of Man, in ten double compartments, boy and man in the ten stages at top, and the ten beasts he is likened to, underneath. Below are verses applying to each age.

"Here after foloweth the ten ages of mankynde lykened be ten dyuers bestis as here is expresly shewed / and how the nature of mankynde dothe chau*n*ge from ten . . . . . tyme of a . . . . . . co . . .

[Cut of] The .X. Ages.

[Fro]M one vnto .x. a childe is he
[Whyp]i*n*ge his toppe *with* sporte & playe
[Lep]yng as y₀ gote right merily.
. . . . s his care bothe nyght & day
[At .xx. yere he is iocond an]d plesand
. . . . t pryde
. . . .
. . . .

¶ At .xxx. yere he is named a man
And syb to the bull of nature stronge
Reue*n*ginge his right where euer he ca*n*
with whome it be bothe short & longe

¶ Nowe forty yere he is ywys
Condicyond as a lyon in euery degre
Which maketh hym often withouten mys
To lese his wysdom beleue ye me

¶ At fifty yere then can he glose
Wily as the forein worde and dede
That euer wyll wynne & neuer lose
& eke of his seruyse he wyl haue mede

¶ At threscore yere he dothe descende
But couetyse in him is rocted than
Euyn as the wolfe he doth amenden
ȳ woroeth the shepe wher euer he can

At .lxx. he is syb to the hownde
ȳ gnaweth yᵉ bone so doth he his hart
All sportes he casteth to the grownde
Lest therfore his sowle sholde smart

¶ At fourscore yere withouten fayle
He is disdayned with man and wyfe
Syb to the Cat that lycketh her tayle
Euer be the fyre that is his lyfe

¶ At fourscore & x he is s . . .
Scorned of man and child h[e is]
From hym is wisdom & st[rength gone
Echone wyll his deth in b

¶ At .C. yere dethe commes . . . . . .
& maketh him as a gose yᵗ i[s] . . .
So plucke yᵒ frendes . . . .
But he in erthe is s . . . . . . "

p. 83. *This worlde is but a vanite.* A later copy of this Poem, with the burden "This world is but a wannyté" was printed by Mr Halliwell for the Warton Club in 1855, in *Early English Miscellanies,* p. 9-12. It has ten stanzas of eight lines each, and winds up with an extra "In Domino confydo. Amen, dico vobis."

p. 88. *Erþe vppon erþe.* In Mr Halliwell's *Early English Miscellanies* from the Porkington MS., Warton Club, 1855, is a later and somewhat different version of this poem in twelve stanzas of six, and two introductory stanzas of seven lines. Mr Halliwell calls the Porkington one "the most complete copy known to exist." It seems a late recast of the old version. Mr Halliwell also notes, p. 94, "Other versions, varying considerably from each other, are preserved in MS. Seld. sup. 53; MS. Rawl. C. 307; MS. Rawl. Poet. 32; MS. Lambeth 853 (in this text); and in the Thornton MS. in Lincoln Cathedral (fol. 279). Portions of it are occasionally found inscribed on the walls of churches."

p. 137. Note to p. 58. The inquirer as to climacterical years is referred to "A Succinct Phylosophical Declaration of the nature of clymaterical yeares occasioned by the death of Queene Elizabeth" in MS. Sloane 2117, fol. 231.

Hymns to the Virgin, Christ, &c.

Veni, Coronaberis.

(A SONG OF GREAT SWEETNESS FROM CHRIST TO HIS DAINTIEST DAM.)

(Lambeth MS. 853, ab. A.D. 1430, page 1.)

Surge mea sponsa, swete in siȝt, ȝ ȝ   *Arise, My beloved, who gavest Me suck*
     And se þi sone þou ȝafe souke so scheene;
þou schalt abide with þi babe so briȝt,
4   And in my glorie be callide a queene.
Thi mammillis, moder, ful weel y meene,   *from thy breasts.*
Y had to my meete þat y myȝt not mys ;
Aboue alle creaturis, my moder clene,   *Above all creatures thou shalt be crowned.*
8   Veni, coronaberis.

Come, clenner þan cristal, to my cage ;   *Come, My dove,*
Columba mea, y þee calle,
And se þi sone þat in scruage   *and see thy son who was made a slave for man.*
12   For mannis soule was made a þralle.
In þi palijs so principal
I pleyde priuyli wiþoute mys ;
Myn hiȝ cage, moder, haue þou schal ;   *Thou shalt have His high place, and be crowned.*
16   Veni, coronaberis.

Daughter of Sion,
spotless flower,

For macula, moder, was neuere in þee ;

Filia syon, þou art þe flour ;

thou shalt sit
crowned by Me,
[Page 2.]
and all My saints
shall honour thee.

Ful sweteli schalt þou sitte bi me,

20 And bere a crowne with me in tour,

¶ And alle my scintis to þin honour

Schal honoure þee, moder, in my blis,

þat blessid bodi þat bare me in bowur,

24 Veni, coronaberis.

Princess of
Paradise, Mother
fair,

Tota pulcra þou art to my plesynge,

My moder, princes of paradijs,

Of þee a watir ful well gan sprynge

the well of mercy
in thee shall bring
thy blessed body
to bliss.
Come and be
crowned.

28 þat schal aȝen alle my riȝtis rise ;

¶ þe welle of mercy in þee, moder, lijs

To bringe þi blessid bodi to blis ;

And my scintis schulen do þee seruice,

32 Veni, coronaberis.

Come, My chosen
one, Maiden
Queen,

Veni, electa mea, meekeli chosen,

Holi moder & maiden queene,

On sege to sitte semeli bi him an hiȝ,

36 þi sone and eek þi childe.

dwell here with
Me in bliss,

¶ Here, moder, wiþ me to dwelle,

With þi swete babe þat sittiþ in blis,

þere in ioie & blis þat schal neuere mys,

and be crowned.

40 Veni, coronaberis.

[Page 3.]
Sweet Mother,
remember the
dew that dropped
from our lips
when we kissed.

Veni, electa mea, my moder swete,

Whanne þou bad me, babe, be ful stille,

Ful goodli oure lippis þan gan mete,

44 With briȝt braunchis as blosmes on hille.

¶ Fanus distillans it wente with wille,

Oute of oure lippis whanne we dide kis,

þerfore, moder, now ful stille,

Come and be
crowned.

48 Veni, coronaberis.

Veni de libano, þou loueli in launche,
þat lappid me loueli *with* liking song,
þou schalt abide *with* a blessid braunche,
52   þat so semeli of þi bodi sprong.

  ¶ Ego, flos campi, þi flour, was solde,
þat on calueri to þee cried y-wys :
Moder, þou woost þis is as y wolde ;
56   Veni, coronaberis.

(margin: Come from Lebanon, thou who sangst Me to sleep,)

(margin: Me who on Calvary cried to thee.)

Pulcra vt luna, þou berist þe lamme,
As þe sunne þat schineþ clere,
Veni in ortum meum, þou deintiest damme,
60   To smelle my spicis[1] þat here ben in fere.
My palijs is piȝt for þi pleasure,
Ful of briȝt braunchis & blosmes of blis ;
Come now, moder, to þi derling dere !
64   Veni, coronaberis.

(margin: Lovely as moonlight,)

(margin: come thou to Me.)

(margin: [Page 4.] My palace is dight with blossoms of bliss. Come, Mother, come and be crowned.)

Quid est ista so vertuose
þat is cuere lastyng for hir mekenes ?
Aurora consurgens graciouse,
68   So benigne a ladi, of such briȝtnes,

  ¶ þis is þe colour of kinde clennes,
Regina celi þat neuere dide mys ;
þus endiþ þe song of greet sweettnes,
72   Veni, coronaberis.

(margin: Who is she that shall endure for ever for her meekness ?)

(margin: The Queen of Heaven, who never sinned. Come thou then, and be crowned !)

[*Quia Amore Langueo*, or " In a tabernacle of a tour," and its continuation " In a valey of þis restles mynde," printed in *Political, Religious, and Love Poems*, pp. 148-150, follow here. Then " Ihesu, þi swetnes," p. 8, and " Ihesus þat sprong, p. 12, of this volume.]

[1] Compare " Awake, O north wind, and come, thou south ; blow upon my garden, *that* the spices thereof may flow out. Let my beloved come into his garden, and eat his pleasant fruits." *Solomon's Song*, ch. iv. 16. " My beloved is gone down into his garden, to the beds of spices, to feed in the gardens, and to gather lilies." vi. 2.

Hail, Blessed Mary!

[*Lambeth MS.* 853, *ab.* 1430 A.D., *page* 24.]

The heavy Clarendon letters mark the red of the MS.

Hail, Mary,
Mother of

HEil be þou, marie, þe modir of crist,
Heil þe blessidist þat euere bare child!
Heil þat conceyuedist al wiþ list

the Son of God!
Maiden, never
defouled,

4   þe sone of god boþe meeke & mylde !
¶ Heil maide sweete þat neuere was filid !
Heil welle and witt of al wijsdome !

fairest flower of
the field.

Heil þou flour ! heil fairest in feeld !

8   **Aue regina celorum !**

Hail, comely
Queen,

Heil comeli queene, coumfort of care !
Heil blessid lady bothe fair & briȝt !

healer of all pain.

Heil þe saluour of al sore !

12   Heil þe laumpe of lemys liȝt !

[Page 25.]
Hail, mother of
Christ,

¶ Heil þou blessid beerde in whom [crist] was piȝt !
Heil ioie of man bothe al and sum !
Heil pinacle in heuene an hiȝt,

the king of Angels.

16   **Mater regis angelorum !**

Hail, fairest of all,
who bred our
bliss, on whom all
women in child-
bed call.

Heil crowned queene, fairest of alle!
Heil þat alle oure blis in bradde !
Heil þat alle wommen on doon calle

20   in temynge whanne þei ben hard bistadde !

All fiends dread
thee, who feddest
thy Son with
maiden milk,
Thou flower of
virgins.

¶ Heil þou þat alle feendis dredde,
And schulen do til þe day of doome !
With maidens mylk þi sone þou fedde,

24   **O maria, flos virginum.**

Heil fairest þat euere god foond,
Whiche chees þee to his owne bour !
Heil þe lanterne þat is ay liȝthond !
28 To þeo schulen loute boþe riche & poore.
¶ Heil spice swettist of sauour !
Heil þat al oure ioye of come !
Heil of alle wommen fruyt & flour !
32 **Velud¹ rosa vel lilium.**

Hail, choice of God,

whom rich and poor adore.

Hall, fruit and flower of womankind.
[1 ? velud ; l, u, and d rubbed]

Heil be þou goodli ground of grace !
Heil blessid sterre upon þe see !
Heil of coumfortis in euery caas !
36 ¶ Heil þe cheeuest of charitee !
Heil welle of witt and of merci !
Heil þat bare ihesu, goddis sone !
Heil tabernacle of þe trynyte !
40 **Funde preces ad filium.**

Hail, Star upon the sea,

chiefest in charity,

tabernacle of the Trinity.

Heil be þou virgyne of virgins !
Heil blessid modir ! heil blessid may !
Heil norische of sweete ihesus !
44 Heil cheefest of chastite, forsoþe to say !
¶ Lady, kepe vs so in oure last day
þat we may come to þi kingdom !
For me & alle cristen þou pray,
48 **Pro salute fidelium.   Amen.**

Hail, blessed maiden,

In our last day bring us to thy realm.

Pray for all faithful souls !

Aue Maria.

[*Lambeth MS.* 853, *ab.* 1430 A.D., *fol.* 26.   *Partly written without breaks.*]

HEil be þou marie, c*ri*stis moder dere,
þ*at* art queene of heue*n*, fair and sweete of chere,
þat art sterre of heue*n* schinyn*g*e briȝt & clere !
4   Helpe me, lady ¹ ful of myȝt, & heere my p*r*aiere
                    Aue maria.

Heil blessid marie, mylde queene of heue*n* !
Blessid be þi name, ful good it is to nempne :
8   To þee, lady, y make my moone ; I p*r*aie þee
                    heere my steue*n*,
    And let me neue*r*e die i*n* noo*n* of þe syn*n*is
                    seuene.
                    Aue maria.

Heil be þou marie þat art flour of alle,
12   As roose in cerbir so reed !
    To þee, ladi, y clepe and calle,
        To þee y make my beed ;
    þou be i*n* stide & in stalle
16   Whanne y schal drawe to deed,
    A*nd* lete me neue*r*e falle
        in boondis of þe queed !
                    Aue maria.

20   **H**eil be þou, marie, þat hiȝ sittist in troone !
    Y biseche þee, swete lady, grau*n*te me my
        boone,

Ihesu to loue & drede, & my lijfe to amcende soone,   amend my life,
And bring me to þat blis þat neuere schal be   and bring me to
    doone.   everlasting bliss.

24   **Aue maria.**

Heil be þou marie, gloriouse moder hende !   Send me meek-
Mecknes & honeste, with abstynence, me sende,   ness and charity,
With chastite & charite into my lyues cende,   that I may go to
28 And þat þoruȝ þi praier, lady, I mote to heuen   heaven.
    blis weende !

                      Aue maria.

[*Oratio Magistri Richardi de Castre*, p. 15, below, follows here.]

Poems to Christ.

The Sweetness of Jesus.

[*Lambeth MS.* 853, *ab.* 1430 A.D., *page* 14.]

Jesu, beside Thy sweetness all

IHesu, þi swetnes, who-so myȝte it se,
And þerof haue a cleere knowynge,

earthly love is bitter.

Al erþeli loue bittir schulde be
4 Saue þin a-loone *without* leesinge.

Teach me

I praie þee, lord, þat lore leere me,
Aftir þi loue to haue longynge,

firmly to set my heart on Thee.

And sadli to sette myn herte on þee,
8 In þi loue to haue most liking.

No earthly love delights like Thine,

So likinge loue in erþe noon is ;
In soule who-so coude him soþeli se,
Him to loue were mykil blis,

the King of Love.

12 For king of loue callid is he.
¶ W*ith* true loue, y wolde þis,
So faste to him bounde be,

I would my heart were wholly Thine.

þat myne herte were holli his
16 So þat no þing likid me but he.

[Page 15.]
If Nature bids me love my kin, I

IF y for kyndenes schulde loue my kyn,
þan me þenkiþ in my þouȝte

should love Thee first, who didst

Bi kyndeli skile y schulde bigynne
20 At him þat haþ me maade of nouȝt.

put Thy likeness in my soul.

¶ His lijknes he sette my soule with-inne,
And al þis world for me haþ wrouȝt,
As fadir he fondid my loue to wynne,
24 For to heuene he haþ me brouȝt.

As moder of him, y make now mynde,
þat bifore my birþe to me toke hede,
And siþen with baptym waischiþ þat kynde
28 þat foulide was þoruȝ adams dede.

¶ With noble mete he norischiþ oure kynde,
For with his fleisch he dooþ us fede,
A bettere fode may no man fynde,
32 To lastynge lijf it wole us lede.

Before my birth He cared for me,

and now feeds our race with His blood.

Oure broþer & sustir he is bi skile,
For he so seide, & lerid us þat lore
þat who so wrouȝte his fadris wille
36 Briþeren & sustren to him þei wore.

¶ Mi kinde also he took þer-tille,
Ful truli truste y him þerfore
þat he wole neuere lete me spille,
40 But wiþ his mercy salue my sore.

He is the brother and sister of

those who do His Father's will.

[Page 16.]
He took my nature, and so I trust Him.

The loue of him passiþ, certis,
Al erþeli loue þat may ben here ;
God & man, my spouse he is,
44 Weel ouȝte y, wrecche, to loue him dere.

¶ Boþe heuen and erþe holli is his,
He is lord of greet powere,
Callid he is þe kyng of blis,
48 His loue me longiþ for to leere.

His love passes all earthly love, and He is my spouse.

His name is King of Bliss.

Aftir his loue me þenkiþ long
For he haþ myne ful dere y-bouȝte ;
Whanne y was wente fro him with wrong,
52 From heuen to erþe he me souȝte.

¶ Mi wrecchid kynde for me he fonge,
And al his nobley he sette as nouȝt,
Pouert he suffride, & peynes stronge,
56 Aȝen to blis or he me brouȝte.

He bought my love full dear,

took my wretched nature, and

brought me to bliss.

[Page 17.]
Love for me
brought Him to
earth,
and for that He
pledged His life,

Whanne y was þral, to make me fre,
Mi loue fro heuene to erþe him ledde,
My loue aloone haue wolde he,
60   For þerfore he leide his lijf to wedde.
    ¶ Wiþ my foo he fauȝte for me,
Woundid he was, and bittirli bledde,

and shed His
precious blood.

His preciouse blood ful greet plente
64   Ful pitcuousli for me was schedde.

His sides were
bloody, His heart
pierced with a
spear.

Hise sidis bloo and blodi were
þat sumtyme were ful briȝt of blee ;
His herte was persid wiþ a spere,
68   Hise ruli woundis were ruþe to se.
    ¶ Mi raunsum forsoþe he paied þere,

He gave His life
for my guilt.

And ȝaf his lijf for gilt of me,
His deeþ schulde be to me ful dere,
72   And perse myn herte for pure pitee.

My heart should
break with pity,

For pitee myn herte schulde breke on two,
To his kyndenes if y took hede ;

for I was cause
of all His woe.

Encheson y was of al his woo,
76   He suffride ful harde for my mis-dede.

[Page 18.]
For me He
suffered death,

    ¶ To lastyng lijf þat y schulde go,
He suffride deeþ in his manhede ;
And whanne his wille was to lyue also,

and rose again,

80   Aȝen he roos þoruȝ his godhede.

and went to
heaven.

To heuen he wente with myche blis
Whanne he ouercome his bataile,

He protects me
from my foes,

His baner ful brode displaied is
84   Whanne so my fo wole me assaile.
    ¶ Weel ouȝte y, wrecche, to ben his,
He is þat freend þat neuere wole faile ;

the friend that
never fails, and
asks only my love
again.

No þing desiriþ he þat is,
88   But true loue aȝen for his trauaile.

Thus wolde my spouse for me fiȝt,
And for me was woundid sore,
For my loue his deep was diȝt;
92 What loue myȝte he kipe more?
¶ To ȝelde his loue haue y no myȝte
But loue him hertili perfore,
And worche weel with werkis riȝt
96 pat he hap lerid me with loueli lore.

For me He was wounded sore, and died.

I cannot repay His love, but

only obey His commands.

Wip loueli lore his werkis to fille,
Weel cuȝte y, wrecche, if y were kynde,
Nyȝt & day to worche his wille,
100 And euere haue pat lord in mynde.
¶ But goostli foos greuen me ille,
And my freel fleisch makip me blinde;
perfore his mercy y take me tille,
104 For betere bote can y noon fynde.

[Page 19.]
I must alway work His will;

but my foes and flesh blind me.

I fly to His mercy,

Betere bote is noon to me
pan to his mercy truli me take
pat with his fleisch hap made me free,
108 And me, wrecche, his childe wole make.
¶ I praie pat lord for his pitee
pat he for synne me not forsake,
But ȝeue me grace fro synne to flee,
112 And him to loue let me neuere slake.

which is my best remedy.

O Lord, forsake me not, but give me grace to love Thee.

Ihesu, for pe swetnes pat in pee is,
Haue mynde of me whan y hens wende,
With stidfast trupe my wittis pou wis,
116 And, lord, pou scheelde me from pe feende!
¶ For pi mercy forȝeue me my mys,
pat wickid werk my soule neuere schende,
And lede me, lord, in-to pi blis,
120 With pee to wone withoute cende. AMEN.

For Thy sweetness

keep me from the evil one!

[Page 20.]
For Thy mercy lead me into bliss, ever to dwell with Thee!

Be my Coumfort, Crist Jhesus!

[*Lambeth MS.* 853, *ab.* 1400 A.D., *page* 20.]

Jesu,

savour sweet to
man's soul,.

    IHesus þat sprong of iesse roote,
    As us haþ prechid þi prophete,
    Flour and fruyt boþe softe and sote,
4 To mannis soule of sauour sweete ;
    Ihesu ! þou brouȝtist man to boote
    Whanne gabriel gan marie greete,
    To felle oure foomen vndir foote,
8 In hir þou siȝ a semeli sete :

thou Virgin's
son !

Son, and Mother,
comfort me!

¶ A mayden was þi modir meete,
    Of whom þou took fleisch for us ;
    As ȝe may boþe my balis beete,
12 So be my coumfort, crist ihesus.

Jesu,

to save man's
soul
thou wert poorly
clad, put in a
cradle,
[Page 21.]

born in
Bethlehem.

    Ihesu, þou art wijsdom of witt
    Of þi fadir ful of myȝt !
    Mannys soule, to saue it,
16 In poore aparaile þou were piȝt.
    ¶ Ihesu ! þou were in cradil knyt,
    In wede wrappid boþe day & nyȝt,
    In bethleem born, as þe gospel writt,
20 With aungelis song and heuene liȝt.

By Thy kiss to
Thy mother,

comfort me!

    Barn y-born of a beerde briȝt,
    Ful curteis was þi comeli cus ;
    þoruȝ uertu of þat sweete siȝte,
24 So be my coumfort, crist ihesus.

Jesu, who wast
fair when young,

    Ihesu, þat were of ȝeeris ȝong,
    Fair and fresch of hide and hue,

Whanne þou were in þraldom þrong,
28 And turmentid with many a iewe,

when Thou wert
on the Cross,

¶ Whanne blood and watir were out wrong,
For beetinge was þi bodi blewe ;

turned'st blue,

As a clot of clay þou were for-clonge,
32 So deed in prouз þanne men þee þrewe.

and like a clod of
clay wast cast in
grave.

¶ But grace of þi graue grew ;
þou roos up quik coumfort to us.

But quickly Thou
arose.

For hir loue þat þis councel knewe,
36 So be my coumfort, crist ihesus.

Then comfort me.

Ihesu, sooþfast god and man,
Two kindis knyt in oon persone,
þe wondir werk þat þou bigan
40 þou hast fulfillid in fleisch & bone.

[Page 22.]
Jesu, God and
man,

¶ Out of þis world wiзtli þou wan,
Liftynge up þi silf a-loone ;

soon Thou rose
from the dead to

For myзtili þou roos, & ran
44 Streiзt vnto þi fadir in trone.

Thy Father's
throne.

¶ Now dare man make no more moone ;
For man it is þou wrouзte þus,

Man shall mourn
no more,

And god wiþ man is maade at oone,
48 So be my coumfort, crist ihesus.

so comfort me.

¶ Ihesu crist, holi and hende,
þat beerde was blessid þat bare þee,
Aftir hir whanne þou gan sende,
52 In heuene blis wiþ þee to bee.

Jesu, Thou
sentest for Thy
Mother to heaven,
and set her higher

¶ Out of þis worlde whanne sche wende,
Boþe bodi & soule were sett in see
Hiзer þan ony of aungelis kinde,
56 In troone a-fore þe trynyte.

than the angels
on a throne.

¶ þere may þe sone his modir se
In heuene an hiз to helpen us ;

[Page 23.]
Peerless Princess,
pray for me !

þou peerless princes, praie for me !
60 And be my coumfort, crist ihesus.

and, Jesus,
comfort me!

Jesus,

       I hesu, my soucreyne sauyour,
       Almyȝti god, þere ben no moo :

rule me,   -

       Crist, þou be my gouernour,
64   þi feiþ lete me not fallen fro.

be my food in
body and soul,

      ¶ Ihesu, my ioye and my socoure !
       In my body and soule also,
       God, þou be my strengist fode,
68   And wisse þou me whan me is wo.

      ¶ Lord, þou makist freend of foo,
       Lete me not lyue in langour þus,

stay my sorrow,

       But se my sorowe, & scie now ' ho,'

and comfort me.

72   And be my coumfort, crist ihesus.

Prince of Peace,
I pray Thee

       I hesu, to þee y crie and greede ;
       Prince of pees, to þee y praye ;
       þou woldist bleede for mannis nede,

help me in all my
fear,
   [Page 21.]

76 And suffre manye a feerdful fray.

      ¶ þou me fede in al my drede
       Wiþ pacience now and ay

let me please Thee
in word and deed,

       Mi lijf to lede in word & dede

and die well at
my day.

80   As is moost plesaunt to þi pay,

      ¶ And to deie weel whanne it is my day.
       Ihesu, þat deied on tree for us,

Be my comfort,
Christ !

       Lete me not be þe feendis pray,
84   But be my coumfort, crist ihesus !   AMEN.

[The two Hymns to the Virgin, " Heil be þou, Marie," printed
on pages 4-7 of this Text, follow here.]

Richard de Castre's Prayer to Jesus.

[*Lambeth MS.* 853, *ab.* 1430 A.D., *page* 28, *written without breaks.*]

Oratio magistri Richardi de castre, quam ipse posuit.

IHesu, lord, þat madist me,
    And wiþ þi blessid blood hast bouȝt,
    Forȝeue þat y haue greued þee
4   With worde, with wil, And eek with þouȝt.

    Jesu,

    forgive what I have grieved Thee.

¶ Ihesu, in whom in al my trust,
    þat deied upon þe roode tree,
    Withdrawe myn herte from fleischli lust,
8   And from al wordli vanyte !

    Withdraw my heart from fleshly lust.

¶ Ihesu, for þi woundis smerte
    On feet & on þin hondis two,
    Make me meeke & low of herte,
12   And þee to loue as y schulde do !

    Make me meek and lowly of heart.

¶ Ihesu, for þi bitter wounde
    þat wente to þin herte roote,
    For synne þat haþ myn herte bounde,
16   þi blessid bloode mote be my bote.

    Thy blood must heal my guilt.

¶ And ihesu crist, to þee y calle
    þat art god ful of myȝt ;
    Kepe me cleene, þat y ne falle
20   In deedli synne neiþer be day ne nyȝt.

    Keep me pure from mortal sin.

¶ Ihesu, graunte me myne askinge,
    Perfite pacience in my disese,
  And neuere mote y do þat þing
24   þat schulde þee in ony wise displese.

Let me never
displease Thee.

¶ Ihesu þat art oure heuenli king,
    Sooþefast god, & man also,
  Зeue me grace of good eendinge,
28   And hem þat Y am holden vnto.

Grant that I and
all to whom I am
bound may die
well.
[Page 20.]

¶ Ihesu, for þe deedly teeris
    þat þou scheeddist for my gilt,
  Here & spede my praiers,
32   And spare me þat y be not spilt.

Speed my prayers
that I may not be
condemned.

¶ Ihesu, for them y þe biseche
    þat wrappen þee in ony wise,
  With-holde from hem þin hond of wreche,
36   And lete hem lyue in þi seruice.

Keep Thy reveng-
ing hand from
those who anger
Thee.

¶ Ihesu, moost coumfort for to se
    Of þi scintis euerychoone,
  Coumfort hem þat careful been,
40   And helpe hem þat ben woo bigoon.

Comfort all who
are full of care.

¶ Ihesu, keepe hem þat been goode,
    And ameende hem þat han greued þee,
  And sende hem fruytis of erþeli fode
44   As ech man nediþ in his degree.

Amend all who
have grieved Thee.

¶ Ihesu, þat art with-outen lees
    Almyзti god in trynyte,
  Ceesse þese werris, & sende us pees
48   Wiþ lastinge loue & charitee.

Stop these wars,
and send us peace.

Ihesu, þat art þe goostli stoon
    Of al holi chirche in myddil erþe,

Bringe þi fooldis & flockis in oon,

52 And rule hem riȝtli wíth oon hirde.

¶ Ihesu, for [1] þi blessidful blood,

Bringe, if þou wolt, þo soulis to blis

For [2] whom y hauo had ony good,

56 And spare þat þei han do a-mys. AMEN.

["Who-so wilneþ," printed on pp. 11-12 of *The Babees Book*, &c., follows here, on p. 30 of the MS.]

Bring Thy flocks and folds in one;

[1 Page 30.] and bring to bliss all who have done me good. Amen. [2 ? *for* Fro]

Do Merci bifore thi Jugement.

[Lambeth MS. 583, ab. 1430 A.D., page 54, written without breaks.]

Our Creator is
the maker of all,

There is no creature[1] but oon,
　　Maker of euery creature,
God a-loone, & euer more oon,
4　And þre in oon alway to endure.

to whom we
lament

¶ To þat lord we make oure moone
　　To whom al coumfort is, & cure,

how frail we are.

To þinke how freel we ben echoon.
8　In þis world is hard auenture :
　¶ Who-so þerof is moost ensure,
　　　Sunnest schal he be schamed and schent.

God, be merciful
before thy
judgment.

Or þou þe world with fier pure,
12　　Do merci bifore þi iugement.

Lord, do mercy or þat þou deeme,
　　Lest þou dampne þat þou hast wrouȝt :

Damn not Thine
own work to
please the Devil;

What ioie were it a feend to qweme,
16　To ȝeue him þat þou hast dere bouȝt.

banish us not
from thy sight.

¶ Out of þi siȝt if þou us fleme,
　　We ben dampned riȝt as nouȝt ;
　þi passioun make us briȝt & schene
20　In wil, in worde, in dede & þouȝt !

---

[1] A later hand has written *our* over the *ure* of 'creature,' and dotted the *ure* out.

¶ For whi, synne haþ us þoruȝ souȝt ;
　　þer-fore ameende þou oure entent
　　To þe doom or we bee brouȝt !
24　　Do mercy bifore þi iugement.

Amend our purposes before Thy Judgment.

We axe þi mercy, þou heuenli king,
　　For þou art lord of ech degre ;
　　Of erþe þou madist oure bigynnynge,
28　　And aftir with spirit enspirid us free.
¶ Wiþ trees and gras þou ȝaf us growinge,
　　Wiþ beestis, feelinge lijf haue we,
　　And with aungils we haue vndirstondinge,
32　　And þerbi we schulden know þee.
　　þou baddist þat alle schulde multiplie,
　　But we ben fals & necligent :
　　For we may not hide us from þin iȝe,
36　　Do merci bifore þi iugement.

[Page 55.]
We ask Thy mercy.

Thou madest us of earth, and breathedst spirit in us,

giving us sentient life with beasts, and knowledge with angels.

We are false, but cannot hide from Thee.
Have Mercy on us !

Þou baddist us axe merci, & we schulden haue ;
　　It dooþ us coumfort on þee to calle,
　　þou hast ordeined man to saue,
40　　For þi merci passiþ þi werkis alle.
¶ þi herte blood for us þou ȝaue,
　　þou madist us free where we were þralle :
　　Lete neuere þe feend oure soulis craue
44　　þat waischen was in þin holi welle !
¶ Oure fleisch is freel, it makiþ us falle,
　　Wiþ grace [1] we risen & schulen repente ;
　　And in hope of þee we schal :
48　　Haue merci to-fore thi iugement.

Thou baddest us ask Mercy.

Thou gavest Thine heart's blood for us :

[1 Page 56.]
our flesh is frail ;
give us Grace and Hope ; and

have Mercy on us.

We axe mercy bi riȝtwijsnes,
　　For þi biheest is al oure riȝt,
　　And of þi greet kindenes
52　　þou hast mercy to us bihiȝt.

We rely on Thy promise of

Mercy to us.
We can do nothing

2 *

of ourselves.

¶ We ne be but erþe watirlees,
    þat to springe vertu haþ no myȝt ;
þis worldis likerose bittirnes
56   Bireueþ us discrecioun & oure siȝt.

The world, the flesh, and the devil fight with us.
Have Mercy before Thy Judgment.

¶ þe feend, þe fleisch, þe worlde, wiþ us ay fiȝt ;
    þus be we taken in turment ;
þerfore, lord, or þi doom be diȝt,
60   Do merci bifore þi iugement.

We have corrupt-ed our nature with sin ;

Wiþ synne we han defoulid oure kinde,
    And kinde may we not eschewe ;
To wraþþe þee, god, we ben vnkinde ;

we are untrue.

64   þou kindeli king, we ben vntrewe !
¶ Aȝens þis can no clerk skile fynde ;
    Graciose god, upon us rewe ;

Remember not our trespass ;
[Page 57.]

Take not oure trespase in to mynde,
68   But in þi doom lete merci sue !

we cannot escape Thee.

¶ For þouȝ we wolden from þee remewe,
    In ech place þou art present ;

Have mercy on us.

Or we were born, lord, þou us knewe ;
72   Do merci bifore þi iuggement.

Lord, we commit our life to Thee ;

Lord ! oure soule, oure spirit, oure lijf,
    Into þin hondis, lord, we bitake ;
Out of temptacioun and strijf,

keep us night and day.
Jesu, drive

76   Lord, kepe us wheþer we slepe or wake.
¶ Ihesu, for þi woundis fyue,
    And for þi modir sake,

the devil from us when we die ;
let him not seize our souls.

þe feend away from us þou dryue
80   Whanne deeþ with us maistrie schal make,
¶ And suffre him not oure soule away to take
    For whiche on roode þou were torent ;

Have Mercy before Thy Judgment.

Aȝens þi doom we tremble & quake ;
84   Do merci tofore þi iugement !

God, mingle Mercy with Justice,

God, þou deeme us riȝtwijsli,
    Medele þou merci with exccusioun,

For wo han forfetid wrongfulli ;

88   Take hedo to oure contricioun !

¶ We zeelde us synful & sory

    By ¹Knowliche & confessioun ;

    þi passioun & þi mercy

92   We take to oure entensioun.

¶ Bileeue is oure saluacioun,

    With keping of þi comaundement.

    God, putte þin holi passioun

96   Bitwixe us & þi iugement !   Amen.

take heed to our contrition.

We are sinful and sorry.
    [¹ Page 58.]

We plead Thy sufferings :

put them between us and Thy Judgment.

["As y gan wandre," printed below, follows here.]

The Love of Jesus.

(Pages 90-102, written without breaks.)

Love in Christ is everlasting life;

Loue is lijf þat lastiþ ay
  þere it is in crist made fest,
Whanne wele ne wo it slake may,
4   as writen han men wisest.

It turns work into rest.

¶ þe nyȝt it turneþ in-to day,
  Traueile it turneþ in to rest :
If þou wolt do as y þee say,
8   þou schalt þanne be with þe best.

¶ Loue is a þouȝt with gret desijr,
  And also of a fair loouynge ;

Love is like a fire;

Loue y likne in-to a fier
12   þat slakeen may for no þing.

It cleanses us of sin.

¶ Loue clensiþ us of oure synne,
  loue oure blis schal bringe,
Loue þe kingis herte may wynne,
16   loue of ioie euere may synge.

The help of Love reaches to heaven.

þe socour of loue is liftid hie,
  For into heuene it ran ;
Me þenkiþ in herte þat it is sliȝe,
20   þat makiþ þe peple boþe pale & wan.

[Page 91.]

¶ þe beed of blis it goiþ ful nyȝ,—
  I telle ȝou it as y can,—
þerof us þenkiþ þe wey to drie,

It couples God to man.

24   For euere loue coupliþ god to man.

¶ Loue is hetter þan þe cole

    To hem þat of it is fayn & frike,

þe flawme of loue, who myȝte it þole,

28   If it were euermore lijke :

¶ Loue us heliþ, & makiþ in qwart,

    And liftiþ us up in-to heuene-riche,

And loue rauischiþ crist in-to oure herte,

32   I woot nowhere no loue it is lijke.

Love is hotter than coal;

It cheers us, and lifts us to heaven.

¶ Leerne to loue if þou wolt lyue

    Whanne þou schalt hens fare ;

Al þi þouȝt to him þou ȝeue

36   þat may þee kepe from care ;

¶ Loke þou þin herte fro him not twynne

    þouȝ þou wandre euery where,

So þou may weelde him with-inne,

40   And loue him hertili euermore.

Learn to Love

God, and put not thine heart from Him.

Ihesu, þat me loue hast lende,

    In-to þi loue þou me bringe,

Take to þee al myn entente

44   þat þou be to me myn ȝeringe,

¶ And þat synne from me awei were went,

    And loue come myn owne coucitynge,

þat my soule hadde herd & hent

48   þe songe of þi sweete louynge.

[Page 92.] Jesu! bring me to Thy Love

that sin may leave me,

and my soul may hear the song of Thy loving.

¶ þi loue is to us euerelastynge

    Fro þat tyme þat we may it verrili fele,

þerinne make we euere brennynge,

52   þat no þing may it uerrili keele.

¶ Mi þouȝt, take it into þin hand,

    And stable þou it ilke a dele,

þat y be no þing hildande

56   To loue uerrili þe worldis wele.

Thy Love lasts ever.

Take my desire to Thee

that I may not love the world.

If I love any
earthly thing,

¶ If y loue ony erþeli þing
        þat paieþ to my wille,
    And sette my ioie in foule likinge,
60   Whanne it may come me tylle

[Page 93.]
at my death it
will be poison

I may drede at my departynge
        þat it wole be attir & ille,
    For alle my welþis ben wepinge

in hell.

64   whanne peyne my soule wolde spille.

Earthly joy,

¶ þe ioie þat men heere seen
        Is ful likinge vnto þe iȝee ;

now fresh and
green, soon fades.

    þat now is fair, freische, and grene,
68   And anoon aftir is welkid awey :

Such is the world;

¶ þis is þe world, alle men moun seen,
        And wole be vnto domysday,

toil and trouble.

    Ful greet traueile, & myche tene ;
72   To flee þat is ful hard in fay.

If you leave evil,

¶ If þou leue yuel in al þi þouȝt,
        And hate þe filthe of synne,

and give yourself
to Christ,

    And ȝeue to him þat þee dere bouȝt,
76   þat he weelde þee with-inne,

¶ Al þi soule þi lord haþ souȝt,
        And þerof he wolde not mynne ;

He will bring you
to bliss.

    þus schalt þou to blis be brouȝt,
80   And wonye henene wiþ-ynne.

[¹ Page 94.]
Love is trusty and
true,

¶ For-¹soþe þe kinde of loue is þis,—
        þere it is trusty and trewe,—
    To stoonde euere in stabilnes,

never changing.

84   And chaunge neuere for no newe.

He who finds it

¶ þat wiȝt þat þat loue may finde,
        Or euere in herte it knewe,

need not care.

    Fro care it turneþ þat kinde :
88   Such a mirþe fyndiþ to fewe.

¶ For-þi, loue þou as y þee rede ;
    Crist is trewe loue, as y þe telle ;
Wiþ aungilis take þou þi stide ;
92   þat ioie loke þou not felle.

Christ is true Love.

¶ In erþe hate[1] þou no maner qweed,
    But loke þat þi loue may dwelle,
For loue is more strenger þan deed,
96   Loue is more harder þan helle.

[1 ? loue]

Let thy Love be His.
It is stronger than death and hell.

¶ Loue is liȝt, & a birþun fyne ;
    Loue gladiþ boþe ȝonge and oolde ;
Loue is wiþout ony pyne,
100   As louers han me toolde.

Love gladdens young and old.

¶ Loue is goostli deli-[2]ciouse as wijn
    þat makiþ men boþe big & bolde ;
To þat loue y schal me so faste tyne,
104   þat y in herte it euermore holde.

[2 Page 95.]
It is delicious as wine.

Hold fast to it.

¶ Loue is þe swettiste þing
    þat heere in erþe men may han ;
Loue is goddis owne derlinge ;
108   Loue byndiþ boþe blood & baan.

Love is

God's own darling.

¶ In loue, þerfore, be oure likinge ;
    I knowe no betere won ;
For me oonli, & my louynge,
112   Loue makiþ boþe but oon.

Let our delight be in it.

¶ But al fleischli loue schal fare
    As dooþ þe flouris of may,
And schal be lastande na mare
116   But as it were an hour of a day ;

Fleshly love is like May flowers,

lasting only an hour.

¶ And sorewen aftir þat ful sare
    Hir lust, her pride, & al her play,
Whanne þei aren cast in care,
120   In-to pyne þat lastiþ ay.

And after comes sore sorrow

in hell.

¶ Whanne her bodies in þe fen liggen,

[Page 96.]
When men rise
again,

    þanne schulen her soulis be in drede,

And up aȝen as men schulen risen,

124   And answere for her mys dede.

If they have sin-
ned here,

¶ If þei be seen þan in synne,

    And now heere þer liif þei ledde,

they shall lie in
hell.

þan schulen þei ligge helle wiþ-inne,

128   And derkenes haue to mede.

Rich men shall
rue their sin in
hell.

¶ Riche men her hondis schal wrynge,

    And her wickid werkes abie

In flawmes of fier bitterli brennynge,

132   Wiþ care and sorewe schamefastli.

But Love, and
then you'll sing
to Christ.

¶ If þou wolt loue, þan may þou synge

    To þi lord crist in melodie :

þe loue of him ouercomeþ al þing ;

136   In loue lyue we & die.

Jesu, Son of God!

Ihesu ! god-is sone þou art,

    lord of moost hiȝ magiste,

send Love into
my heart!
[¹ Page 97.]

Sende verrili loue in-to myn herte

140   Oonly ¹ to coueite þee !

¶ Reue me likinge of þis world,

Be my Love!

    Mi loue þat þou may be ;

Take myn herte in-to þi ward,

144   And sette þou me in stabilte !

Jesu, maiden's
Son!

¶ Ihesu ! þou, þe maidens sone,

    þat with þi blood me bouȝte,

Pierce my soul
with thy spear.

þirle my soule with þi spere anoon,

148   þat myche loue in men hast wrouȝt.

¶ Me longiþ þou lede me into þi siȝt,

    And fastne þere in þee my þouȝt ;

Make my heart
light in Thy
sweetness.

In þi swetnes make myn herte liȝt,

152   þat al my woo wexe to nouȝt.

¶ **I**hesu, my god & my loueli king !
　　Forsake þou not my desijr ;
　　Mi þouȝt make to be meekinge ;
156　　I hate boþe pride & ire.
　¶ þi wil is al my desirynge ;
　　Of loue kyndele þou þe fier,
　　þat y with þi sweete louynge
160　　Wiþ aungils take myn hire.

¶ Wounde þou myn herte wiþ-inne,
　　And weelde me at þi wille ;
　　Of blis þat neuere schal blynne,
164　　þou fastne me þat y not spille.
　¶ þat y þi loue may wynne,
　　Of grace my þouȝt þou fille,
　　And make me cleene of synne
168　　þat y may come þee tille.

¶ Ihesu ! putte in-to myn herte
　　þe memorie of þi pyne !
　　In lijknes, and eek in qwarte,
172　　þi loue be euere myne !
　　Mi ioie is al of þee ;
　　My soule, take it as þine ;
　　Mi loue euere wexinge be,
176　　So þat y neuere dwynne.

¶ My loue is euere in siȝinge
　　While y dwelle in þis way ;
　　Mi loue is in þee longynge,
180　　þat bindiþ me niȝt & day
　¶ Tille y come vnto my king,
　　þere y wone with him may,
　　And se his fair schynynge
184　　In lijf þat lastiþ ay.

Jesu, my God !

make me meek ;

kindle within me
the fire of Love!

Wield me at Thy
will

[Page 98.]
that I may win
Thy love

and come to Thee.

Jesu, remind me
of Thy sufferings,

give me Thy
Love,

take my soul as
Thine.

My Love sighs

and longs

till I come to my
King

in Life that lasteth
aye.

¶ Longinge is in me so lent
    For loue, þat y ne can lete ;
His loue he haþ me now sent
188   þat euery bale may bete ;
¶ Siþen þat myn herte was brent
    In cristis loue so sweete,
Al woo fro me awei is went
192   And we neuere aȝen schulen mete.

¶ I sitte and synge of loue longynge
    þat in my ¹ brest is now bred.
Ihesu, my king and my ioiynge !
196   Whi ne were y to þee led ?
¶ Ful weel y woot in al my ȝernynge,
    In al ioie, y schulde be fed.
Ihesu ! me brynge to þi woniynge,
200   For þe blood þat þou hast bleed.

¶ Demed he was on a crosse to heng,
    þe fair aungelis foode ;
Wiþ scourgis þei gan him sore swing
204   Whanne þat he bounden stoode ;
¶ His brist was bloo in betyng,
    Not spilt was his blood ;
þe þorn crowned þat king
208   þat doon was on þe roode.

White was his nakid breest,
    & reed his bloodi side,
Wan was his face fairest,
212   Hise woundis depe & wide.
¶ þe iewis wolde not þan reste
    To pyne him more in þat tide ;
Al he suffride þat was wisest,
216   His blood to lete doun glide.

Christ has sent me His Love. / All woe has left me. / I sit and sing. [¹ Page 99.] / Jesu, my joy, / bring me to Thy dwelling. / Jesus was hung on the Cross, / scourged, / and crowned with thorns. / White was His breast, [See Political R. and L. Poems, p. 214.] wan his face, / down his blood did glide,

¶ Blyndid were hise faire yȝen,
    And al his fleisch bloodi for-bete ;
    Hise ¹ louesum lijf þat alle men siȝe[n],
220   Ful myldeli he out gan lete.

out he let his
[¹ Page 100.]
lovesome life.

¶ Deed & lijf bigunne to striuen
    Wheþer myȝt be maister þere ;
    Liif was slayn, & roos a-ȝen ;
224   In-to blis ful fair may we fare.

Life was slain,

but rose again to
give us bliss.

¶ He þat þee bouȝt haue al þi þouȝt,
    And lede he it in to his loore ;
    Ȝeue al þin herte to crist in qwarte,
228   And so to loue him euermore.

Give thy heart to
Christ !

¶ I siȝe, y sobbe, boþe day & nyȝt,
    For oon þat is so fair of hue ;
    þere is no þing myn herte may liȝt
232   But his loue þat is so true.

I sigh and sob for
Him ;

nothing but He
can comfort me.

¶ Who so hadde him in his siȝte,
    Or in his herte him knewe,
    His moornynge schulde turne into ioie briȝt,
236   His longynge into glewe.

He alone can

turn mourning
into joy.

¶ In mirþe lyueþ he nyȝt & day
    þat loueþ þat sweete childe ;
    Wraþþe wolde from him awey,
240   Were he neuere so wielde.

He who loves
Jesus,

¶ It is ihesu, forsoþe to say,
    Of alle meekist & myelde ;
    He þat in herte him loueþ þat day,
244   From yuel he wole him schielde.

[Page 101.]

meekest and
mildest of all,
will be shielded
from evil.

¶ Of ihesu þanne moost list me speke,
    þat may of al my bale be bote ;
    Me þinkeþ myn herte wole al to-breke
248   Whanne y þinke on þat soote.

Of Jesus I must
speak,

for He has caught
my heart in Love.

¶ In loue lauȝt he haþ my þouȝt,
  þat y schal neuere for-lete ;
Ful dere me þinkeþ he haþ me bouȝt,
252 Wiþ bloodi heed, hondis, & feete.

For Love my
heart will burst
when I see Christ.

¶ For loue myn herte wole to-berste
  Whanne y þat fair loue biholde ;
Loue is ful fair þere it is fest,
256 þat neuere wole be coolde.

¶ Loue us reueþ þe nyȝtis rest ;
  In grace it makiþ us boolde ;

Love is the best
of all works.

Of alle werkis loue is þe beeste,
260 As holi men me haþ tolde.

I sigh when I
think on Jesus

¶ No wondir if y siȝhande be,
  And siþen in woo al bi-sett ;

nailed on the
Cross,

Ihesu was nailid upon þe tree ;
264 ȝhe, al bloody for-beet.

¶ To þinke on him is greet pitee,
  To se how tenderli he gret ;

[Page 102.]

þis haþ he suffride, man, for þee,

suffering for man.

268 If þat þou wolt þi synnes leett.

The sweetness of
Christ's Love
none can tell.

¶ þere is no lijf in erþe may telle
  Of þis loue þe swetnes :
þat stidefastli in loue can dwelle,
272 His ioie is euere cendelees.

God keep him
who Loves, from
hell.

¶ God schielde þat he schulde to helle,
  þat of loue longinge kan not ceesse,
Or euere hise enemyes schulde him qwelle,
276 Or þat he so his loue schulde lese.

Jesus is the Love
that lasteth aye.

¶ Ihesu is þe loue þat lastiþ ay ,
  To him is oure longinge.
Ihesu þe nyȝt turneþ to day,
280 And derknes in-to day spryng.

¶ Ihesu! þinke on us now and ay,
 For þee we holde oure kyng!
 Ihesu, ʒeue us grace þat weel may,
281 To loue þe with oute eendynge!—A-M-E-N.

Jesu, think on us,

and give us
Grace to love
thee ever. Amen.

["The good wijf," printed in *The Babees Boke*, &c., follows.]

Se what oure Lord Suffride for oure Sake.

[Pages 117—120, written without breaks.]

Make good cheer
in Christ's name.

BOthe ȝonge & oolde, wheþir ȝe be,
    in cristis name good cheer ȝe make,
and liftiþ up ȝoure hertis, & se

See what he
suffered for our
sake.

4   What oure lord suffride for oure sake.
as meeke as ony lombe was he,
    ensaumple of him weel mowe we take,

Like Him let us
suffer too.

& to suffre also in oure degre,
8   & in his seruice euere to wake.

If friends forsake
us, let us think

And if oure freendis forsake us heere
    so þat we be left al aloone,

on Jesus,

þinke on ihesus þat bouȝt us dere,
12   & to him make we al oure moone ;
¶ For of þat lord weel may we leere
    What wrong he suffride among hise foon ;

how all his
disciples fled but
Mary and John.

Whanne hise disciplis fledden for feer,
16   þer bood no mo but marie & iohne.

If wrong be
wrought us,

If ony wrong to us be wrouȝt,
    Be it in word eiþer in dede,

God may help at
need ; think how
    [Page 118.]
Christ has bought
us with His
blood.

Be of good hope ȝit in þi þouȝt
20   How god may us helpe alle at neede,
And þinke we how ihesus crist us bouȝt,
    & for oure synnis hise blood wolde blede ;
for his owne gilt was it nouȝt,
24   for he dide neuere synful dede.

¶ If wickid men do us defame,
    þinke how crist was bouȝt & solde ;

If men defame us,

to suffre for him is no schame,

let us suffer for Christ,

28   but him to serue loke we be boold.
And if men hurte us in oure name,
    We must forȝeue, boþe ȝonge & olde,

an l forgive.

For þouȝ we suffre myche blame,

He suffered 1000 fold more.

32   crist suffride moore a þousand foold.

And of pouert þouȝ we wolde playne,

If poverty pinch us,

    for þat we wanten worldli good,
þinke we on ihesu, þat lord souereyn,

think how Jesus hung, poor, on the Cross,

36   how pore he heng upon þe roode,
¶ And how he stryued not ageyn,
    but euere was meeke & mylde of mood.

meek and mild.

to folewe þat lord we schulden be fayn,

Follow Him.

40   in what degre þat euere we stood.

& þouȝ we haue sorowe on ech side,

If sorrow come, and wrong,

    & al aboute wrong & woo,
ȝit suffre meekeli, & a-bide,

still suffer meekly and think on Jesus
[Page 119.]

44   And þinke on ihesu þat suffride also,
and how he was in ful greet drede,
    Vnto hise peynis whanne he schulde go ;
he suffride moore in hise manhede

who suffered more than any man.

48   þan euere dide man, or euere schal do.

¶ þouȝ we with wrong to deeþ be brouȝt,

If we be wrongly brought to death,

    ȝit suffrraunce is a sikir way
For þe loue of ihesu þat us dere bouȝt

yet suffer still

52   & deide for us on good friday ;
Wherfore us þinkiþ in oure þouȝt
    þat we oure lord schulde please & pay,

and please our Lord.

And we to sette þis world at nouȝt,
56   And suffre we wickid men to say.

In ihesu crist was meekenes moost,

Christ, through meekness, overcame

    And þerfore he þe maistrie hadde,

and bound the
Devil,

And boond þe feend for al his boost

60   þat he was neuere so sore adradde.

¶ Al aȝens his wil & al his oost

and brought
Adam, Eve, and
others, from hell.

Adam & eue *with* him he ladde,

And many moo out of þat coost

64   þat weren in *pri*soun ful hard bistadde.

If you follow
Jesus,

And if þou in ihesu haue delite,

þouȝ al þe world do þee assaile,

[¹ Page 120.]
you shall find that
Meekness will
prevail,

Do aftir þis, & þou schalt wite

68   þat meekenes ¹ Wole þee moost availe ;

For who þat suffriþ heere dispite,

And meekeli a-bidiþ *in* þat bataile,

bringing you to
endless joy.

it wole turne hem to greet profite

72   & eendlees ioie for her trauaile.

If any man do
you wrong,

¶ If ony man do to us a mys,

Or wole in ony wise to us offende,

for Jesus' love

for þe loue of ihesu haue my*n*de on þis,

76   & lete meekenes þi mood ameende

. wiþ ihesu *crist*, as oon of his,

suffer it ; you
shall dwell with
Him in bliss.

And suffre meekeli what god wole sende,

þanne schal we be w*ith* him in blis

80   þat euere schal laste wiþouten eende. A-M-E-N.

["How mankinde dooþ bigynne," pp. 58-78 of this Text,
follows here.]

I wiȝte my silf myn owne Woo.

[*Lambeth MS.* 853, *ab.* 1430 A.D., *page* 226-33.]

IN my ȝonge age ful wielde y was,
Mi silf þat tyme cowde y not knowe,
Y wolde haue my wil in euery place,
4 *And* þat haþ now brouȝt me ful lowe.
þinke, ihesu, how ȝ am þin owe !
For me weere þi sidis boþe pale & bloo !
To chastise me þou doist it, y trowe ;
8 Y wiȝte my silf myne owne woo !

In my youth I
was very wild,

and that has
brought me low,
But, Jesu, think
how I am thine.

I blame myself
for my woe.

¶ I made couenaunt, true to be,
Firste whanne y baptisid was ;
Y took to þe world, & wente from þee,
12 Y folewide þe feend al in his traas ;
From wraþþe and enuye wolde y not pas ;
Coueitise and auarise y usid also,
Mi fleische hadde his wille, alas !
16 Y wiȝte my silf myn owne woo !

I kept not my
baptismal
covenant,

but followed the
devil,

let my flesh
have its will,

¶ Now y woot y was ful wielde,
In þat my wil passid my witt ;
Y was ful sturdy, & þou ful myelde ;
20 Ihesu, lord, y knowe weel it.
Of þi blis y were ful qwytt
If y hadde aftir þat y haue do ;
But to þi merci y truste ȝitt,
24 Y wiȝte my silf myn owne woo !

and was
rebellious.

But, Jesu,
[Page 227.]

I trust to Thy
mercy.

3 *

I was proud and extravagant,

¶ I was hiȝ of herte and stowte,
    And in my cloþing wondre gay ;
    I lokide men schulde vn-to me lowte
28 Where-so þat y wente bi þe wey.

caring only for women and dress.

    Faire wommen, and good aray,
    Al myn entent y took þer-to ;
    Aȝen þi techinge euere y seide nay ;
32 I wite my silf myn owne woo !

I trusted riches, not God,

¶ I trustide more to worldli good
    þan to god þat it me sente ;
    Weelþe made me hiȝ of mood ;
36 Lust and likyng me ouer wente.

and stuck at no-thing to get money.

    To gete good y wolde not stente,
    Y ne rouȝte how y come þer-to ;
    To þe poore y neiþer ȝaf ne lente ;
40 Y wiyte my silf myn owne woo !

·[Page 228.]
Lord, I feared Thee not,

but Thou

¶ Lord, y hadde no drede of þee ;
    Mi grace wente away þerfore ;
    But, lord, as þou bouȝtist me,
44 So lete me neuere be for-lore.

suffered'st for me.

    For me þou suffredist peines sore ;
    þou art my freend, and y þi foo ;

Have mercy on me!

    Mercy, lord ! y wole no more ;
48 Y wiyte my silf myn owne wo !

Three evil things ruin a man.

¶ þer ben .iij. poyntis of myscheef
    þat ben confusioun to many a man,
    Which þat worchen to her soulis greet greef ;
52 Y schal hem rehersen as y can.

1. The desire of poor men to look like rich ones.

    Poore men proud, þat litil han,
    þei wolen be a-raied as riche men goo ;
    þei hindren hem silf & oþir þan,
56 And mowe wiȝte hem silf her owne woo.

II. The covet-ousness of rich men,

¶ A riche man, þeef, is anothir,
    þat of coucitise wole not slake ;

If he with wrong bigile his broþir,

60 Heuene blis he schal forsake ;
Bifore god, for þeefte it is take,
Al þat with wrong he wynneþ so ;
But if he here a-meendis make [1]
64 he schal wiyte him silf his owne woo.

che.ting others,

[Page 229.]
which with God
is theft.

[1 MS. made]

¶ An oolde man lecchour, þe þridde it is,
For his complexioun wexiþ coolde ;
It bringeþ þe soule to peyne from blis,
68 It stinckeþ on god so manye foolde.
Theise .iij. þat y haue of toold
Ben pleasinge to þe feend oure foo ;
Hem to use, who is so boold,
72 May wiyte him silf his owne woo.

III. The lechery
of old men.

These three please
the Devil.

¶ Manye defautis god may fynde
In vs þat schulde hise seruauntis be ;
He schewith us loue, & we vnkinde,
76 Certis þe more to blame be wee.
Summe staren broode & moun not se,
Synne is þe cause it fariþ soo ;
Suche dreden not god, y seie to þee,
80 And may wiyte hem silf her owne woo.

God shows us

love, and we look

away from Him
through sin.

We may blame
ourselves for our
own woe.

¶ In iij. þingis y dare weel sayn
god schulde be worschipide ouer al þing ;
do riȝtwijsnes with merci with al þi mayn ;
84 þe þridde is cleennesse in lyuynge :
To bischopis & curatis þat han kepinge,
it is her charge, & to lordis also.
and if þei contrarie god-is biddinge,
88 þei may wiyte hem silf her owne woo.

[Page 230.]
In three things
we should
worship God,
Righteousness,
Mercy,
Chastity,

which bishops,
curates, and lords
are bound to keep.

¶ wrong is an hiȝ seete þere riȝt schulde be,
merci for mys deede is putt away ;

Wrong is now set
up where Right
should be.

Lechery drives
away Purity.

letcherie haþ made clennesse to flee,

92   Loue may not abide nyght ne day.

þus þe feend, y dare weel say,

Man, amend, or
blame yourself
for your own
torment.

wole make oure freend *oure* moost foo :

man, amende þee whilis þou may,

96   Or wiyte þi silf þin owne woo.

I must be trou-
bled while I fol-
low my own will.

¶ It is no wondir þouȝ y be woo

myn owne wil while y wole sewe,

& my lordis bidding wole not doo :

100   y am ful fals, but he is trewe,

And ȝit he fyndiþ me *with* al þing newe,

[Page 231.]
I serve the devil.

And y serue þe feend, and go him froo;

But if y amende, it schal me rewe,

104   And may wiyte my silf my*n* owne woo.

¶ In þre degrees þe world kept is,

Priests, knights,
and labourers
shall all suffer if
they do wrong,

With preestis, knyȝtis, and laborere,

And which of hem þat doon amys,

108   þei schulen it abie wondir deer.

Bi good ensau*m*plis þe *pre*estis schuld lere

þe vnleerned how þei schulden doo :

and blame them-
selves for their
distress.

If her word & werk coorde not in fere,

112   þei mowe wite he*m* silf her owne woo.

Lords should

¶ Knyȝthode also, lordis, ne oþir,

Schulden not be of conscience light,

help the poor,

þei schulde*n* helpe her poore suste*r* or broþe*r*,

116   And also strengþe hem in her ryght

but instead often
oppress them, and
when in woe will
have to blame
themselves.

þoruȝ pride & coueitise summe leesen he*r* myȝt ;

For letcherie, grace is kept he*m* froo ;

If þei biholde her owne in-syght,

120   þei mowe wiyte he*m* silf he*r* owne woo.

[Page 232.]
Labourers should

¶ þe laborer schulde truly traueile þan,

And be riȝtful boþe in worde & deede,

And what-euere werkis þat he can,

124 And resonabli to take his meede.

Wrongfulli summe her lijf heere lede,

Among leerned & lewde it is founde so,

And in her laste eende it is to drede

128 þei mowe wiyte hem silf her owne wo.

work well, and take reasonable wages. But some do wrong,

and will have to blame themselves.

¶ Man, take hede whot þou art :

But wormes meete ! þou woost weel þis ;

Whanne þat þe erþo haþ take his part,

132 Heuene and helle schal haue his.

If þou doist weel, þou goist to blis ;

If þou do yuel, þou goost to þi foo ;

Loue þi lord god, & þinke on þis,

136 Or þou wite þi silf þin owne woo.

Man, worms' food, thou must go

to bliss or hell.

Do not have to blame thyself for thy woe.

¶ Now ihesu crist, oure sauyour :

From oure foos þou vs defende ;

In al oure nede be oure socour,

140 Heere & whanne we hens wende,

And sende us grace so to amende,

His blisse þat we may come vnto,

Heere to make so good an eende

144 þat wee not cause oure owne woo.

Deo gracias.

Christ, defend us,

here and hereafter.

[Page 253.]

Bring us to Thy bliss that we may not cause our own woe.

[End of the MS. In a later hand is " This is sir Hary
myndes booke, Record of John Dauis, & of sir John George & of
Sir Robert george fines (?)]

[Page 88.]

This name, Jesus,

when thou speakest it, it shall be honey in thy mouth and melody in thine heart.

[2 Page 89.]

Think on Jesus;

it drives out the devil, and opens heaven.

Also hail Mary often.

Keep Love in thine heart, for Love is the fulfilling of the Law.

IF þou wole be weel with god, And haue grace to reule þi lijf, And come to þe ioie of loue, þis name ihesu, fastne it so fast in þin herte þat it come neuere
4 out of þi þou3t. And whanne þou spekist to him, & seist ihesu poru3 custum, It schal be in þin cere ioie, And in þi mouþ hony, And in þin herte melodie, For þou schalt þinke ioie to heere þe name of
8 ihesu be nempned *,² swetnes to speke it, Myirþe & song to þinke on it. If þou þinke on ihesu contynueli, And holde it stabli, It purgiþ þi synne, it kyndeliþ þin herte, It clarifieþ þi soule, It remeueþ
12 anger, it doiþ a-way slownes, It wyndiþ in loue fulfillid of charite, It chasiþ þe deuel, it puttiþ out drede, It openeþ heuene, it makiþ contemplatijf men haue in mynde ofte ihesu, For alle vicis &
16 fantums it puttiþ fro þe louer. Also þerto heile ofte marie boþe day & ny3t, And þanne myche ioie & loue schalt þou fele. And þou do aftir þis lore, þe neediþ not greetli coueite many bookis. Holde loue
20 in herte & in werk, And þou hast al þat we may seie or write, For fulnes of lawe is charite: In þat hongiþ al.

* There is a curl of contraction as for er over the second e.

A Song Called

Þe Deuelis Perlament,

or

Parlamentum of Feendis.

(*Lambeth MS.* 853, *ab.* 1430 A.D., *Pages* 157—182.)

Whanne marye was greet w*ith* gabriel,
  And had conceyued & bore*n* a childe,
Alle þe deuelis of þe eir, of erþe, & of helle,
4 helden þer paralame*nt* of þ*at* maide mylde,
¶ What man had made her wombe to swelle.
  " To tempten hir ȝe tenden to seelde ;
  her childis fadir who can telle,
8 Who dide w*ith* hir þo werkis wielde ? "

¶ In helle þe feendis þoo answeride,
  " We knew neu*er*e fadir þat he hadde,
  But amongis prophetis we haue leerid
12 þat god w*ith* man haþ couenau*nt* maade :
  ¶ A serpent i*n* deseert was rerid,
  So schal god-is sone in man be had,
  þe soule of hi*m* schal be vnsperid,
16 his herte to-cloue, and he for-bleed.

¶ þese prophetis speken so in myst,
  What þei mente we neu*er*e knewe ;
  þei spoken of oon schulde hote c*ri*st,
20 But maries sone hiȝte ihesu ;

When Mary had
given birth to
Jesus, all the
Devils held a
consultation as to
who had begotten
Him.

The Hell-Devils
did not know, but
had learnt from
Prophets

that God's Son
was to be raised
in man, and to
suffer death ;

[Page 158.]
and that one,
Christ, should
come ; but Mary's
Son was Jesus.

Also that Christ
should be one
with God; but
Jesus was not. So
the Devils were
puzzled.

¶ And þei seiden þat crist wiþ god schulde be
   a-twist,

But þis ihesu neuere in þe godhede grew ;

We ben bigilid alle wiþ oure lyst.

24   þe clooþ is al of anothir hew ;

But they agreed
that if God sent
His Son into
man's body,

¶ And þouȝ god make hise perlament

Of pees, mercy, trouthe, & resoun,

And from heuen til erþe his sone be sent

28   In mankinde to take a cesoun,

¶ We schulen ordeyne bi oon assent

A priuey councell al of tresoun,

they would claim
Him as theirs,
because He'd be
of man's nature,

And clayme ihesu for oure rent :

32   For þat he is kinde of man, it is good chesoun.

¶ Write we his name, wheþer we spede,

Siþen to us he is vnknowen,

and though of
alien begetting,
yet sown in
Adam's ground,
   [Page 159.]
and to be reaped
by them,
God notwith-
standing.

For þouȝ he be come of straunge seed,

36   ȝit in adams grounde was he sowen.

¶ Whanne he is ripe, do we oure dede ;

Loke we þat we him boþe repe & mowen,

For þouȝ god him silf oure rollis rede,

40   Bi riȝt we chalenge ihesu for oure owne."

The Master Devil
undertook to
tackle Jesus,

"To me, maistir deuel, it lijs ;

To ihesu wole y take hede,

To norische him in manye delijs,

44   His freel fleische boþe to cloþe & fede ;

¶ And þouȝ þat he be neuere so wijs,

ȝit out of þe wey y wole him lede,

make a fool of
him, and bring
His soul to hell.

And make of him boþe fool and nyce,

48   And in helle his soule brede."

¶ þus deuelis þer wilis caste

For 30 years they
tried

Wiþ þer argumentis greete,

& þritti ȝeer þei foondid faste

52 To tempte ihesu in manye an hete.

¶ " In to a wildirnes with ihesus y paste,
Of him knowliche for to gete,
And fourty daies þere he faste
56 Wiþoute sleep, drinke, or meete."

to tempt Jesus, and went to a wilderness where

he fasted 40 days.

¶ þe maistir deuel wondre þou3te
Of ihesus stalworþe complexioun ;
Bi mannys fode lyuede he nou3te,
60 But bi praiers and deuocioun.
¶ " But whanne he bigan to hunger, as me þou3t,
To tempte him þanne y made me boun :
' Lo, heere be stoonys hard y-wrou3te,
64 Make herof breed, y seide, to mannis foisoun.'

[Page 160.] The Master Devil wondered at Jesus' constitution, living only on prayers; but at last tempted Him, 'Here are stones, make them bread.'

¶ ' Forsoþe,' ihesu seide, ' not oonli in breed
is verrili mannis propir lyuyng,
But in euery worde of þe godhede
68 To body and soule is coumfortynge.'
¶ Vpon an hi3 pinnacle þanne y him brou3te,
And left him þere, and leep a-downe,
And seide, ' saue þee harmelees, lyme & heed,
72 And kiþe now maistries while þou art 3onge.

Jesus said, 'Man's food is not bread alone, but every word of God.' The devil took Him to a pinnacle, leapt down, and asked Him to follow,

¶ If þou be god-is sone, lete se ;
Of þee is writen longe a-goon,
' Aungils in hondis schullen beere þee
76 Lest þou spurne þi foot at a stoon.'
¶ Quod ihesu, ' in holi writt þou maist se,
Tempte not þi lord god lyuynge aloone ;
Wiþ al þi myght and þi pooste
80 þou schalt him serue, and oþir noone.' "

'Angels shall bear Thee in their hands lest Thou strike Thy foot against a stone.'

[Page 161.] Jesus said, ' Tempt not thy God, but serve Him with all thy might.'

¶ þe deuel si3 it myght not geyn ;
Of ihesu his purpos he gan mys ;
He brou3te him til an hi3 mounteyn,

Then the Devil brought Him to a mountain,

84 And bad him do as he wolde wys.

showed Him all the world's riches, and said,

¶ And þere he schewide him upon þat pleyn,
  Iewels, ritchesse, and worldli blisse ;

'Worship me, and all this is Thine.'

  "Worschipe me here, & bicome my swayn,
88 And y schal ȝeue þee al this."

'Begone, Satan, from heaven !

¶ "Go, sathanas ! from blis þou flit,
  From heuene riche, þat rial tour !
  It is writen oonli in holi writt

Thy Lord God only shalt thou honour.' Alas, said the Devil,

92 'Þi lord god þou schalt honour.' "
¶ "Alas," quod þe deuel, "where hast þou þat
          witt ?

I am sore hit, I never stood such an attack.

  Þi wordis are bittir, þi werkis aren sour,
  Þi conclusioun so soore me knyt,
96 I abood neuere so scharp a schour."

[Page 162.]
Again the Devils held their Parlia- ment in the mist. 'Some one is coming to rifle our home. Once his name was John the Baptist, then Jesus, then Christ.

¶ Þe deuelis gadriden þer greet frame,
  And heelden þer perlament in þe myst.
  "Oon wolde riflee us at hame,
100 And gadere þe flour out of oure gryst ;
¶ Neewe gilours wolde waite us schame,
  Oon[ys] men clepid him iohne þe baptist,
  But now he haþ turned, ihesus is his name :
104 Þat first hiȝte ihesu, now is clepid cryst,

He has never sinned in lust,

¶ I siȝ him neuere rage ne plawe,
  But euere in stabilnes he is ay,
  And streitely kepiþ god-is lawe,

but has resisted temptation.

108 And stijfly wiþ-stoondiþ myn assay ;
¶ To werkis of vice wole he not drawe ;

He said he would throw down the Temple, and raise it on the third day.

  A wondir worde y herde him say,
  Þe greet temple he wolde doun þrawe,
112 And reise it aȝen on þe þridde day.

At His birth

¶ Whanne he was born, wondris bifel :
  Ouer al was pees, boþe eest and west,

In rome of oile þere sprong a welle,
116 From tristiuer to tybre it ran prest.

¶ In rome þer templis doun felle,
þer mawmetis diden al to-brest,
Aungils to scheperdis glorie gan telle—
120 ' In erþe, to al mankinde, boþe pees & rest.'

¶ þe emperour in rome stood hiȝe,
þre sunnis in oon he siȝ schyninge clere,
In þe myddis of hem a maiden he siȝe
124 A man childe in her armes beere.

¶ þe emperour & eek sibile spoken prophesie,
And þei acordiden boþe in feere,
And seiden ' god-is sone mankinde schulde bie ;
128 It is þe tokene, þe tyme neiȝeþ neere.'

¶ Also þre kingis come fro fer,
To worschipe ihesu al þei souȝte ;
þat reisid croudis herte þere
132 þem to slee, for þei so wrouȝte.

¶ Bi þe liȝtnynge of a sterre,
To ihesu alle þre presentis þei brouȝte ;
Homeward an aungil tauȝte hem neere
136 A-noþer wey þan þei had þouȝte.

¶ þanne y councellid croud with-inne a while
To distroie þe former prophesie,
þat alle men children in towne & pile
140 to slee þem, þat ihesus myght with hem die.

¶ He ascapide in to egipt ; in þat while
þer mawmetis fil doun from an hiȝe ;
he knew my þouȝte, & siȝ my gilce,
144 y myghte not hide me from his yȝe.

¶ To tempte ihesu it wole not availe ;
Of þe worldis good haþ he no neede ;

a well of oil sprang up in Rome ; temples fell ; idols broke. [Page 163.]

Angels announced Peace on earth to all mankind.

The Emperor saw three Suns in one ; in their midst a Maid with a child.

He and the Sibyl prophesied, 'God's Son shall redeem mankind ; the time draws nigh.'

Three Kings came from far to worship Jesus,

led by the light of a Star, bringing presents

[Page 164.] The Devil advised Herod

to slay all the male children,

but Jesus escaped into Egypt,

detecting the Devil's guile.

' It is no good to tempt Him ;

I leese on him so myche trauaile,

the more I work
the worse I speed

148 þe more y so worche, þe worse y spede ;

¶ With þe scharper a-sautis y him assaile,

þe lasse of me he stoondiþ in drede,

and the less He
heeds me.

þe bolder in bikir y bidde him bataile,

152 þe lasse of me he takiþ hede.

If I tempt Him

¶ For if y tempte him in wraþþe or pride,

Wiþ pacience and mekenes he sconfitiþ me ;

to lechery, He
escapes by
chastity.

If y tempte him to letcherie, y muste me hide,

156 He voidiþ me of wiþ chastitee.

[Page 165.]
He abides in
charity, and will

¶ In glotenie & enuye wole he not abide,

But is euere in mesure and in charitee ;

not be covetous.

In coucitise & auarise wole he not ride,

160 but is euere in largenes and in pouerte."

I can't make him
stumble. He

¶ þe deuel seide, "neiþer in hoot ne coolde

I may not make him stumble ne falle ;

never went to
school, and yet
I saw Him argu-
ing against all
the Doctors.

I nyste him neuere goo to scolee,

164 And ȝit oonis y siȝ him spute in þe scoole halle :

¶ He satte him silf on þe hiȝest stoole,

And argued aȝens þe maistris alle ;

Summe callid him wijs, summe callid him foole,

He calls Himself
God's Son.

168 But 'goddis sone' he him silf dooþ calle.

He makes the
crooked straight,

¶ Hise werkis passen mannis kinde,

For crokid & creplis he makiþ riȝt ;

For deef, & dombe, & boren blynde,

gives sight to the
blind, sense to
madmen,

172 he ȝeueþ hem speche, heeryng, & sight.

¶ Woode men, he ȝeueþ hem þer mynde,

And makiþ mesels hool and liȝt ;

and drives out
devils.

A legioun of feendis in a man he dide finde,

176 Alle he drofe out þoruȝ his myght.

[Page 166.]
He turns water
into wine ;

¶ Wiyn of watir he makiþ blyue,

And dooþ manye a wondir dede,

Wiþ two fyschis, and loues fyue,

180 fyue þousand men y sawȝ him fede.

¶ Tweluc leepis of releef þerof dide þriue
To men, women, & children, þat hadden nede ;
Deed men he reisid from deeþ to lyue,

184 And ȝit weriþ he neuere but oo wede.

¶ He handliþ neiþer money ne knyf,
Neiþer in synne desiriþ he ony woman to kis ;
But oonis he saued a weddid wijf,

188 In spousebriche þat hadde doon mys.

¶ He is so wondirful in lijf,
I can not knowe weel what he is ;
I wolde we hadde cendid oure striif ;

192 He is oute of oure bookis, & we out of his.

A fitte. Siþen y him first tempte bigan,
I siȝ him neuere chaunge hewe ;
Oonys he bad me " go, foule sathan ! "

196 Euere-more þat repreef y rewe.

¶ In werkis he is good, in persoone a man ;
Lijk to him y neuere noon knewe.
Where lerned he al þe witt þat he can ?

200 For euery day he dooþ wondris newe.

¶ I folewide him oonys to a place,
To a mounteyne upon an hiȝte ;
Petir, iames, & iohñ, þere was,

204 Ely & moyses stood þere up riȝt.

¶ I wolde haue seen ihesu-is face,
But y myȝt not, it schoon so briȝt ;
In þe soopfast sunne closid it was,

208 þe briȝt beemys blent my siȝt.

¶ To lette þe prophesie soone y went,
þe iewis to slee ihesu y ȝaf hem chois ;

Marginal notes:

feeds 5000 men with two fishes and five loaves,

leaving 12 baskets of fragments,

and raises the dead to life.

He desires no sin with woman,

and yet once saved an adulteress.

He is such a wonder I cannot make out what He is. He is out of my books.

I have never seen him change colour, though once He reproved me.

[Page 167.] In person He is a man ; but where does His knowledge come from ?

Once I saw Him with Peter,

James, John,

Elias, and Moses.

His face shone so bright

that it blinded me.

I gave the Jews the choice of killing Jesus.

If he dies on the
cross we are
ruined; so I was
sorry to hear
their 'Crucify
Him,' and set
Pilate's wife to
stop it.

If he die on þe roode, we schul be schent :

212   I wolde not þat þei hadde ȝeue þat vois.

¶ Me was woo for þat iugement,
      Of " crucifuge" to heere þe noise ;
      Pilatis wijf y bad bisily ȝeue tent

216   þat ihesu were not doon on þe crois.

[Page 168.]
But the Jews bore
false witness,

and nailed Him on
the Cross till He
died.

¶ Ȝit þe iewis, for hise dedis goode,
      Fals witnes vpon him þei berid,
      And nailed him upon þe roode,

220   And peyned him þere til þat he deied.

I looked sharp
after His soul,

but couldn't see
where it went.

¶ Vndir his lift side y my silf stood,
      And aftir his soule ful naruȝ a-spied ;
      I wist neuere whidir it ȝode ;

224   Whanne he it up ȝaf, so manly he cried ;

The sun and moon
lost their light,
the earth
trembled,

¶ þe sunne & moone losten þer light,
      þe clementis fouȝten as leit of þundir,
      þe erþe qwoke, and mounteynes an hight,

228   Valeis, & stoonys, bursten a-sundir ;

dead men arose.

¶ Dede men risen þoruȝ his myȝt
      To bere witnes of þat wondir ;
      My mynde failid, y loste my siȝte,

I lost my senses,

232   I nyste how soone y came þer vndir.

and don't know
where His soul is
gone to.

¶ Ihesu is soule is wente, y woot not where,
      So priuely it dide from me passe ;
      Whanne his herte was þirllid with a spere,

236   þanne wyste y weel who he was.

[Page 169.]
But we must get
ready all our
tackle, for He'll
attack us.
Prepare for
defence.

¶ Ordeyne we us wiþ al oure gere,
      For hidir he þinkiþ to make a race ;
      Arise we alle þat ben bounden heere,

240   And foond we to defende oure place,

If He comes we
must all try

¶ For if þat he wole hidir come,
      We schulen foonde euery-choon,

Alle to-gidere, boþe hool & some,

244   To teer him from þe top to þe toon."

¶ þanne seide lucifer anoone,

   " It is but waast to speken so ;

   þe spirit of him is now hidir come

248   For to worchen us alle woo."

to tear Him from top to toe. Lucifer said, 'That's no good ; His spirit is now here to work our woe.

¶ þere as þe goode soulis diden in dwelle,

   þei cheyned þe ȝatis, and barred hem faste ;

   " A ! now," ihesu seide, "ȝe princis felle,

252   Openeþ þe ȝatis þat euere schal laste,

¶ And letiþ in ȝoure king of blis to helle."

   þe deuelis axid him þanne in haste,

   " Who is þe king of blis þou doost of telle ?

256   Wenest þou to make us alle a-gaste ?"

The Devils chained up and barred the gates where the good souls were. Jesus said, 'Princes fell, open the gates, and let the King of Bliss into Hell.' The Devils asked, 'Who is the King of Bliss ?'.

¶ " Strong god and king of myght,

   I am lord and king of blis,

   Ouer-comer of deeþ, myghti in fight !

260   Euerlastynge ȝatis, openeþ wight !

¶ Boþe pees, mercy, trouþe, & right,

   I brouȝt them at oon, & made þem to kis ;

   Euerlastynge ȝatis, openeþ on hight,

264   And lete in ȝoure king to take out his !

[Page 170.] 'I am,' said Christ, 'and over-comer of death. Everlasting gates ! open quickly. Let in your King to take out His own.

¶ For y, þe soule of ihesu crist, am come hider,

   Witnes þerof, my body in erþe lieþ deed,

   And þe holi goost with þe soule togider

268   þat neuere schal parte from þe godhede.

¶ In heuen blis ȝe stooden full slidir ;

   þoruȝ pride ȝe offendid my fadris bede ;

   Mannis soule for meeknes schal come þider,

272   þere as ȝe feendis forfetid þat stide."

I, Christ's soul, am here, though my body lies dead. Ye lost Heaven from Pride. Man through Meekness shall possess your seats.'

¶ þanne seide lucifer, " god dide forbede

   To adam in paradiis but oon tree,

Lucifer said, 'God condemned

Adam to Hell for
ever.
[Page 171.]

And peyne of deeþ to haue for þat dede,

276   And aftir in helle euere for to be :

¶ And þou art come of adam seed,

Thou art of
Adam's seed, and
we claim Thee.
There is no return
from Hell.'

þerfore bi right we chalenge þee,

For in holi writt þou made rede,

280   ' In helle is no remedie.' "

'True,' said
Christ; 'but the
closed Hell is for
you; this Hell is
free.

¶ Ihesu seide, " lucifer, sooþ þou tellist me ;

But þou woost not þi silf how

þere is a boonde helle, but þis is free.

284   þe boond helle was ordeyned for ȝou ;

Man is redeemed.

¶ For þat þat man forfetid þoruȝ a tree,

þoruȝ a tree aȝen bouȝt is he now.

Thou art
condemned.

þou madist him synne, þe peyne longiþ to þee,

288   For þou waitist neuere good to mannis prowȝ.

I sprang not from
sinful seed, but

¶ Lucifer, þou me vndir-nome,

And seidist y was of þe seed of adams kyn ;

forsoþe y out of þe godhede come,

took flesh in a
maiden sinlessly.

292   And took fleisch & blood a maiden with-inne.

¶ for as of þe seed of erþe þer springiþ blome,

So mette we, & partid wiþoute synne :

þin argument is fals, so is þi doome ;

296   Bi what right woldist þou me wynne ?

[Page 172.]
When thou
temptedst Adam,

¶ Who was cheef of þi councell

In heuen whanne þou forfetidist þe blis ?

In paradiis adam þou dedist assaile,

300   And temptidist him to forfete his ;

I fought for him,

¶ And y in his quarel took bataile

Aȝen my fadir to amende his mys,

and now will
defeat thee.'

Wherfor of þi purpos þou schalt faile,

304   forthi þi quarel nouȝt it is."

Lucifer said,

¶ þanne lucifer answeride ageyn,

" Whi spekist þou so to me heere ?

It is but wantowne wordis in veyn ;
308 I trowe þou comest hidir us to fere.

¶ Sumtyme whanne y was in heuen an hiȝ,
    þat þat y þere loste for my pride, certeyn,
    Heere-aftir y hope ful sikirly
312 For to come to þat blis ageyn."

¶ Crist ihesu spak to sathan tho,
    And seide to him in þis manere,
    " It is but waast to speken so,
316 Or ony suche wordis to seie now here.

¶ þat tyme while þou in heuen were,
    Ful myche ioie haddist þou tho ;
    For alle þi felawis, glad were þei þere,
320 But riȝt soone it was ouer-goo."

¶ Lucifer spak to him ageyn,
    And seide to him with wordis sere,
    " In þis place y haue dwellid in woo & peine
324 Moore þan þis .iiij. þousand ȝere :

¶ Helpe me to þat blis ageyn
    þe which y loste for my pride þere,
    for þere it is myrie in certeyn
328 To wonye wiþ rial aungils clere."

¶ " I seie þee, lucifer, y schal þee telle,
    Or euere ony þing was wrought—
    Heuene or erþe, eir or helle,—
332 Forsoþe þoo y made þee of nought.

¶ In heuen whanne þou stoodist in wele,
    I made þee aboue aungils alle,
    But þerof rauȝt þou neuere a deel,
336 Suche pride in þin herte gan falle.

¶ In heuen whanne þou were at þi wille,
    þou myȝtist haue be in pees & reste ;

4 *

Marginal glosses:

'Thou comest here to frighten us.

I hope to get to heaven again.'

Christ answered,

'That is idle talk.

[Page 173.] While you were in heaven you had much joy, but it soon ceased.'

Lucifer said, 'I have dwelt here in torment above 4000 years; help me to bliss again, to merry time with angels.'

Christ answered,

'Before the heavens were I made thee of nothing,

and set thee above the angels.

[Page 174.] In heaven

I gave thee my
seat when I went
away, and when
I came back thou

I took þee my seete ful stille,

340   It to þeme þou were ful prest ;

    ¶ And while y wente where me list,

      And come aþen a-noon in hiþe,

said'st thou wast
the worthier,

      þou seidist þat þou were worþiest,

344   And to sitte þere as weel as y ;

and thou never
repentedst.

    ¶ And þou repentidist þee neuermore,

      But euere aggregidist þi trespas.

Adam did; he

    Adam wepte & siþede soore,

asked mercy. God
sent me here for
that, and let me
die.

348   And askid mercy & oile of grace ;

    ¶ My fadir sende me hidir þerfore,

      Vpon a tree leete deeþ me chase,

      A spere þoruþ myn herte gan boore,

352   & leete out þe derworþiest oile þat euere was.

In His name, open
your gates.'

    ¶ In my fadris name of heuene

      Opene þe þatis aþens me ! "

Like lightning
the gates burst.

    As liþt of leite, and þundir leeme,

356   þe þatis to-burste, and gan to flee ;

Christ took
out Adam and all
His chosen ones;
and all sang
thanks, namely,

    ¶ God took out adam and eue ful euene,

      And alle hise chosen companye.

      þe prophetis seiden with mylde steuene,

360   "A song of wondris now synge we."

Adam,

    ¶ "A, ha !" seide **Adam**, "my god y se ;

      He þat made me wiþ his hond ! "

Noah,

    "I se," seide **noe**, " where comeþ hee

364   þat sauede me boþe on watir & londe ! "

Abraham,

    ¶ Quod **abraham**, " y se my god so free

      þat sauede my sone fro bittir bande ! "

Moses,

    þo seide **moyses**, "þese tablis he bitook me

368   His lawe to preche and vndirstande ! "

David,

    ¶ Quod **Dauid**, " we spoken of oon so grym

      þat schulde breke þe brasen þatis. "

Quod **Zacharie**, " & his folk out nym,

372   And leue þere stille þo þat he hatis."

¶ Quod **symeon**, " he liȝtneþ his folk in dym,

Lo where derknes schendiþ her statis.

þo seide **iohne**, " þis lomb, y spak of him,

376   þat al þe worldis synne a-batys."

Zachariah,

Symeon,

and John the Bap-tist.

¶ Oure lord them took bi þe hond,

And brouȝt þem to þe place of blis,

And seide to them, y vndir-stonde,

380   " þis bargeyn y haue bouȝt her, þis :

¶ For riche & pore, free and bonde

þat wole axe grace and ameende þer mys,

Schulen be with ȝou heere pleyande

384   In my kingdom, heuene blis."

[Page 176.] Christ led them to bliss, say-ing he had bought it for all who will

ask grace, and amend their sins.

¶ Thus ihesus crist harewide helle,

And ledde hise louers to paradijs :

Of þe opere hellis wolde he not melle,

388   Where feendis blake bounden lijs,

¶ And where dampned soulis euere schulen dwelle

þat wolen not do weel, but euere be nyce,

Turmentid with horible deuelis of helle

392   þat sumtyme were aungils of prijs.

Thus Christ harrowed Hell. But the other hells he wouldn't touch, where fiends and damn-ed souls ever dwell,

tormented by horrible devils.

¶ Helle repreued þo þe deuel sathan,

And horribli gan him dispice,

" To me þou art a schrewide captayn,

396   A combrid wretche in cowardise."

¶ þo seide lucifer, " siþen þe world bigan

I haue brouȝt hidir manye a greet price

Hidir into helle of al kinde of man,

400   Boþe þe false, foolis, and þe wise.

Then Hell re-proached Satan with cowardice.

[Page 177.] But Lucifer justi-fied himself; he had brought all kinds of men there,

¶ Helle, so worschipide neuere þou were

If þou cowdist haue kept þee soo ;

and Christ too ; but Hell wouldn't

I brouȝte þec boþe god & man in fere ;
404   Whi were þou so nyce to leete him go ?"

¶ Quod helle, " not wiþ þi poowere
I myȝte not werne him oon of tho ;
IIe took out alle þat were him dere ;
408   I myȝte not lette him, þouȝ he wolde mo."

¶ Quod belsabub, " y barrid ful faste
þe ȝatis with lok, cheyne, bolt, & pyn ;
And with oo word of his wyndis blaste
412   þei broken vp, and he came ynne.

¶ He boond me, and downe me caste ;
it is to us no bote to stryue with him ;

Whanne þe dreedful doome is come & paste,
416   Oure eendelees peyne is þanne to bigynne."

¶ þouȝ þe iewis dide ihesu to die,
ȝit on þe þridde day he roos to liif aȝen ;
It was to him moore victorie
420   þan þowȝ he hadde alle þe iewis sleyn.

¶ Summe were glad whanne þei him siȝe,
Summe were sory, summe were fayne,

And sumtyme in oon companye
424   Amonge .v. hundrid he was seyn.

¶ Of oynement ful manye a drope,
Marie mawdeleyne to ihesu sche brouȝte ;
Ihesu wente fro a litil a-slope,

428   And seide, " mawdeleyn, towche me nouȝt."
¶ Alle hise disciplis weren in wanhope ;
For to coumforte them ihesu þouȝte,
And bad hem hise woundis handle & grope,
432   " I haue fleisch & blood ! so spiritus haue nouȝt."

¶ Thomas was of right hard bileeue
Til he hadde spoke wiþ ihesu tho :

Ihesu spak wiþ wordis breue,

436   " Come hidir, thomas, & speke me to ;

¶ For here þou maist now þe sooþe preue,

    How þat y on þe roode was y-doo ;

    And he þat wille not on it bileeue,

440   Schal be dampned to peine for euermo."

Jesus said,
'Come and see
the proof that I
was crucified.
[Page 179.]
He who will not
believe it shall be
damned.'

¶ þanne seide ihesu wiþ myclde speche

    To hise disciplis, " y wole ȝe goo

    To alle creaturis aboute, to preche

444   Myn uprisynge, to freende & foo ;

· ¶ And þo þat bileeuen þat ȝe teeche,

    Bodies and soulis saued ben thoo ;

    And þo þat bileeuen not, y seie to eche,

448   þo schulen for euere to peine goo.

To His disciples
He said, 'Go and
preach my upris-
ing to all people.

They who believe
it shall be saved;
they who do not
shall go to hell.

¶ From ȝou, feendis schulen flee for my name ;

    Eddris & venym schal from ȝou steele ;

    þouȝ ȝe drinke poisoun, it schal not ȝou tame,

452   Neiþer harme ȝou, ne noo greef feele.

¶ I schal newe tungis in ȝou frame

    Alle maner of langagis forþ to deele ;

    And þo þat ȝe touche, sike or lame,

456   Body and soule y wole hem heele."

Devils shall flee
from you,
poison shall not
hurt you.

You shall speak
all languages, and
heal all sick you
touch.'

¶ Oure lord, aftir his resurreccioun, here

    In erþe he was forsoþe dwellynge

    Til hooly þursday comen were,

460   þat he stiȝ to heuene, where he is king.

¶ At þe dreedful doom, wiþ-out lesing,

    Boþe quycke and deede þere schal he deme.

    God ȝeue us grace in oure lyuynge

464   To serue oure god, & marie to qweeme.

[Page 180.]
Christ remained
on earth till Holy
Thursday, and
then ascended
into heaven.
He shall judge the
living and dead.

¶ Of alle þe children þat euere were borun,

    Saue oonli crist him silf a-loone,

Next to Christ

the holiest child
was John the
Baptist, who
baptized Christ

Was no on so holi here biforn

468   As was þis holi child seynt iohun

¶ þat baptisid oure lord in flom iordon

Wiþ ful deuout & good deuocioun,

And after for ihesus loue to deeþ gan goon,

and died for Him. 472   And suffride ful mykil passioun.

Christ's blessed
Mother was

¶ Now schal y telle with ful good cheere

Of þat holi assumpcioun

Of his blessid modir dere,

taken up to her
Son
[Page 181.] 476   How sche was taken up with greet deuocioun

¶ Vnto hir blessid sone, as his wil were,

by angels, and
crowned

þat þerto sente hise aungils a-down,

& vp þei baren þat maiden cleere ;

Queen of Heaven, 480   Queene of heuen þere þei dide hir crowne.

while all the
angels sang

¶ þenne alle aungils þat were in heuené

Were at þe crownyng of þat maide free,

And songen alle with mylde steuene

Glory to God. 484   " Gloria tibi domine."

May we all see
that sight !

¶ þat is a song of ioie and blisse !

God ȝeue us grace þat siȝt to se,

Of his mercy þat we nouȝt mysse,

488   Qui natus es de virgine.

This song is
called ' The
Devil's Perla-
ment,' and is read
on the first Sunday
in Lent. He who

¶ þis song þat y haue sunge ȝou heere,

Is clepid ' þe deuelis perlament :'

þerof is red in tyme of ȝeere

492   On þe first sunday of clene lent.

would go to
heaven must keep
clear of the devil.

¶ Who-so wole haue heuen to his hire,

Kepe he him from þe deuelis combirment ;

In heuene his soule may þere be sure

496   Wiþ aungils to pleie verament.

[Page 182.]
There is no tri-
fling in this tale.

¶ þis lessoun was made but late ;

þere ben no triflis in þis tale ;

þe deuelis boost þus gan he bate,
500   Oure curteis crist, oure king riale.

¶ He helpe us in alle at heuene ȝate,
Wiþ seintis to sitte þere in sale!
Crist! kepe us out of harme and hate,
504   For þin hooli spirit so special!

Explicit parlamentum of feendis.

[The *Diatorie* printed in *The Babees Boke*, &c., follows here.]

The Mirror of the Periods of Man's Life,

OR

BIDS OF THE VIRTUES AND VICES FOR THE
SOUL OF MAN.

[Lambeth MS. 853, ab. 1430 A.D., pages 120-150, written
without breaks, till near the bottom of p. 131, as marked by the
insetting of the even lines here.]

Man's birth is
wonderful! Be-
gotten in sin,

HOw mankinde dooþ bigynne
　　is wondir for to scryne so ;
　In game he is bigoten in synne,

endangering his
mother's life.

4　　þe child is þe modris deedli foo ;
　Or þei be fulli partide on tweyne,
　　In perelle of deeþ ben boþe two.

Poor he comes;
poor he goes.

　Pore he come þe world with-ynne,
8　　Wiþ sorewe & pouert oute schal he goo.

In wyntir nyȝt or y wakid,
　　In my sleep y dreemed so ;

I dreamt I saw
a new-born child
[¹ Page 121.]

　I saw a child modir ¹ nakid,
12　　New born þe modir fro.

go into the desert,
and be taken in
hand by an
Angel-friend and
an Angel-foe.

　Al aloone, as god him makid,
　　In wildirnesse he dide goo,
　Til two in gouernaunce it takid,
16　　An aungel freende, an aungil foo.

The *World* told
the Child it gave
him food and
clothes.

Quod þe world to þe child, " how many foolde
　　Hast þou brouȝt richesse ? now late se :
　þou schuldist deie for hunger and coolde
20　　But y lente meete & cloþe to þee :

I wole þee fynde til þou be oolde;
 How wolt þou quyte it me?"
Quod desteine, " he is bouʒt & soolde."
24   Quod deeþ, " his eende make schal we."

How would he
pay it for them?

Quod þe child, "y come poore þe world with-
 inne
To pursue a wondirful eritage :
Nakid out of þe wyket of synne,
28   Of the perellis of streite passage,
To seke deeþ y dide bigynne,
 þat ilke dredful pilgrymage,
Mi body & soule to parte a tweyne,
32   To make a deuourse of þat mariage.

The Child.
I came to seek
a wondrous
heritage ;

to seek Death ;

to divorce my soul
from my body.

Liʒtnesse, strenþe, corage & bewte,
 þe comaundementis þat god bede ;
Lust, liking, & iolite,
36   .vij. werkis of mercy [1] and þe crede.
Veyne glorie, flaterynge, and vanyte,
 Sowowe, siʒing, loue, & drede,
To the child her seruice profren he,
40   For helle peyne or heuene meede.

Bodily gifts, and
God's Command-
ments,
the Pleasures of
this life, its
[1 Page 122.]
Sorrows, and the
Works of Mercy,

offer to lead the
child to heaven or
hell.

Thanne come oon & stood ful stille,
 And his seruice profride he :
" þese folke wolde þi silfe spille
44   To make þee bonde ; y wole make þee free.
þei han þee tauʒt boþe good & ille ;
 From her councel fast þou flee,
For my name is freewille ;
48   Leue alle hem & folowe me."

Freewill says,

I will make thee
free ;

leave all others,

and follow me.

The ʒonge childe in studie stood,
 And in herte wittis souʒte.
Conscience mengid his mood,
52   " Mi fair childe, what hast þou þouʒt?

Conscience says,

I am Conscience, knowe yuel & good,
    We two to rekenynge must be brou3t :
Biwaare ! free wille wole make þee woode ;
56   Free wille withouten witte is nou3t.

For my name is Conscience ;
    To knowe me þou must bigynne ;
Discrecioun is my science,
60   Vicis & Vertues ¹ to voide a twynne.
A-queynte þe weel with Prudence,
    He lediþ alle vertues out & inne ;
Bi waar of richelees, for he wole make diffence,
64   For he is leder of al synne.

¶ Whanne þe child was .vij. 3eer olde,
    Passyng sowkyng of milke drewis,
þe good aungil þe childe dide weelde ;
68   Al vertu to him þan soone he schewis :
" To fadir & modir honour þou 3eelde ;
    Loue god, & drede, and be of good þewis."
þe wickid aungil bad him be boold
72   To calle boþe fadir & modir schrewis.

Þe good aungil badde him " be mylde
    From al woo, it wole þee werre :
þat man may hi3e housis bilde
76   þat his tunge can weel for-beerre."
Quod þe wickid aungil, " while þou art a child,
    With þi tunge on folk þou bleere ;
Course of kynde is for 3ouþe to be wilde,
80   To beete alle children, and do hem deerre."

Thus at ¹ vij. 3eer age childhood bigynnes,
    And folowith folies many foold ;
Aftirward his childhode blynnes ;
84   Whanne he is fourtene 3eer olde,

know evil from good ; Freewill will make thee mad ; know me, Conscience ; [¹ Page 123.] cultivate Prudence ; beware of Recklessness. At seven years old the Child is urged by the Good Angel to honour his parents ; by the wicked Angel to despise them ; by the Good to bridle his tongue ; by the Wicked to give it license. [¹ Page 124.] Childhood lasts from seven to fourteen.

þanne knowliche of manhode he wynnes,
    þe .vij. vertues wiþ him wonne wolde ;
þanne comeþ þe .vij. deedli synnes

88   With þe wickid aungil housholde to holde.

Then the Seven Virtues and the Seven Mortal Sins strive for the boy's soul.

Quod resoun, " in age of .xx. ȝeer,
    Goo to oxenford, or lerne lawe."
Quod lust, " harpe & giterne þere may y leere,

92   And pickid staffe & buckelere, þere-wiþ to plawe,
    At tauerne to make wommen myrie cheere,
    And wilde felawis to-gidere drawe,
And be to bemond A good squyer

96   Al nyȝt til þe day do dawe.

About twenty years old, Reason advises man study ; Lust advises music, staff-play, women, and wild companions.

Quod conscience, " þat axiþ coost ;
    þe moore þou spendist, þe lesse þou hast ;
þi tyme, þi leernynge boþe ben loost,

100   þi freendis good þou spendist in waast."
Quod lust to conscience, " ȝouþe so muste ;
    ȝouþe can not kepe him chast."
" Good conscience, goo preche to þe post,

104   þi councel saueriþ not my tast.

Conscience says these will waste time and learning.

Lust poohpoohs that ; and the [Page 125.]

young Man scorns it ;

Þouȝ Conscience bidde me be stille,
    I wole holde forþe þat y bigan ;
Al my lust y wole ful-fille,

108   I wole spare no womman ;
Conscience wolde binde me to skille,
    And make me his bondman.
Fareweel Conscience ! weelcome frewille !

112   I wole lerne no more good þan y can."

his lust will spare no woman ;

he will not be a servant to conscience, but to Freewill, and learn no good.

Now vicis & vertues wole not slake,
    Now man is .xx. wyntir in age :
Quod pride, " no man þou forsake,

116   I wole þee sette in þe hiȝest stage."

After twenty years old, come the advice of Pride,

Gluttony,

Quod glotenye, " ny3t & day þou wake ;
    Ete late & eerli in outrage."

Lechery,

Quod leccherie, " þi seed richelees þou schake,

120   And make no force of no mariage."

Wrath,

Quod wraþþe, " loke þou bere þee bolde ;
    What man þee teene, His heed þou breest."

Envy,

[¹ Page 126.]

Quod enuie, " þi foote þou holde,

124   And pursue ¹ for to passe þe beest."

Sloth,

Quod slouþe, " in 3ouþe, or þou be oolde,
    Leerne for to take þi reest."

Covetousness,

Quod Coueitise, " wynnen y wolde."

Avarice.

128   Quod auarise, " locke me in þi cheest."

Pride says, wear
long pockets, and
slashed (?)
clothes ;

" **A**pparaile þe propirli," quod Pride,
    " Loke þi pockettis passe þe lengist gise ;
Slatre þi clothis boþe schorte & side

132   Passinge alle oþere mennis sise ;

reverence no one,

And where þat þou goo ouþer ride,
    Do no reuerence to foole ne wise ;

oppress the poor,
despise advice.

Late no poore nei3bore þryue þee biside ;

136   Alle oþer mennis councel loke þou dispise."

Meekness says :
Pride will bring
you to woe.
Once he was
lovely in highest
heaven,

" **B**i waar," quod Meekenes, " how pride dooþ
        wys ;
He 3eueþ but woo & wyssche to wage ;
Of aungelis bewte þe prijs was his ;

140   In heuene on þe hi3est stage,
He wolde haue peerid with god of blis ;
    Now is he in helle moost looþeli page.
þat feendis forfetid for her mys,

now he is loath-
some in hell,
and meek man
has his inherit-
ance.

144   Is now meeke mannis eritage."

Wrath advises:
meddle in every
quarrel,
[Page 127.]

Quod wraþþe, " From þat councel flee,
    þou art stalworþe, 3onge, and li3te,
Of all quarellis medle þou þee

wrong or right.

148   Boþe of wronge & of ri3te.

Who dar bete þee, nay lete be,
    Riche or poore, weike or wiȝte,
Loke þou bere þee boolde on me,

152   And y for þee wole chide & fliȝte."

Þanne up stood Paciens,
    "As wrappe biddiþ, do not soo,
For wrappe haþ no Conscience,

156   He makiþ ech man operis foo;
þer-with he getiþ his dispence,
    þat schulde be freende, to make hem foo.
Praie god, he be þi diffence,

160   þat þou be not founde in þe noumbre of þoo."

Quod enuie þanne, "y wole þee leere
    To make þi lord to þee tame;
Be homeli, & rowne in his eere,

164   And bringe trewe folk in fals fame.
Make him þi suget, to þee to swere
    þat he schal not discure þi name;
So make him fals witnesse to bere,

168   And gete þee richesse wiþ god-is grame."

Þanne up roos a souereyn uertu
    þat is clepid Charite:
"Loke þou not hise maners sue,

172   For god-is enemy soþeli is he.
Do þou to euery man þat is due
    As þou woldist he dide to þee."
Quod Coueitise "and alle folk were trewe,

176   Manye a man schulde neuere þee.

Caste þee faste to Coueitise,
    Make sotil þi wittis, & forge wilis,
And preue þat trewe men be nyce,

180   For so þe fals þe trewe bigilis;

Such ben worschipid & holden wise,

and so grow rich.

> þei purchasen hem townes, maners, & pilis,

And truþe wolde wite where þi lordschip lijs ;

184   Make heggis bi-twene ȝou, and no stilis."

*Bounty in Alms-
deeds* says, Give to
the poor,

Quod largenes in almesse dede,

> "Coueitise councelliþ þee amys.

Ȝeue to þe pore, & þou schalt spede

188   þe bettir, þe gospel seiþ þis ;

and at the
Judgment

For at þe doome þere þou schalt drede,

> Crist wole reherse of þee y-wys

þe werkis of merci, as clerkis reede :

you'll go to bliss. 192   If þou hast doon hem, þou goost to blis."

Gluttony says,
Love your belly,

"**M**an, loue þi wombe," quod Gloteny,

> " Leie mete upon meete, & ete faste ;

But leue not þi crummes drye,

eat and drink; 196   Drinke þou til þe ful flood be paste.

fornicate, and
never fast.
[Page 129.]

Leue clennesse, & use harlotrie,

> But neuere a day loke þou ne faste ;

In þi wombe make þi tresorie, ·

200   Of þeeuis þanne þou schalt not be agast."

Moderation says,
Gluttony makes

Quod Mesure, " man ! haue me in mynde.

> God made man suget to resoun :

men beasts, and

Wat turneþ a man to beestis kinde

204   But etynge & drynking out of sesoun ?

drunkenness
blinds their souls.

Drunkelew folk ben goostli blinde ;

> For faute of witt her lijf is gesoun ;

In ydil oopis wasten þei her wynde :

208   To repreue suche, god fyndiþ enchesoun."

Sloth says, Never
go to church,
don't mind good
advice,

Quod Slouþe, " bisynesse y þee forbede ;

> To chirche neiþer goo ne renne ;

Who techiþ þee good, take noon hede,

212   Aȝens oo worde ȝeue him ten :

Seie 'alle folk ben not sotil in dede ;'
　Excuse þee so bi oþer men,
And ȝeue hem myche maugre to mede
216　þat ony good þee wolde kenne."

excuse yourself by others' example.

Quod Besinesse, "man ! of Slouþe be waare ;
　He is assigned to helle for synne ;
In good lyuynge þi wittis ware,
220　To drede god þou muste bigynne ;
þi fleischeli lustis þou muste spare,
　For vicis and vertues wole voide atwynne ;
In besinessis hous is good weelfare,
224　And Slouþe haþ hunger and cloþis þinne."

Business warns man against Sloth.

Fear God, and deny your lusts.

[Page 130.]

Business brings welfare.

Quod leccherie to man, "loue þanne weel me,
　þi lustis with wommen þou fulfille,
For if þou in ȝouþe sparist þanne þee,
228　þou maist falle in greet perille.
Ȝouþe ful of corage wole be ;
　þou muste haue helpe, or ellis spille ;
Spare no womman, y councelle þe,
232　þouȝ summe cryen neuere so schille."

Lechery says : Satisfy your lust with women ;

youth will be gay.

Spare no woman.

Quod Chastite to man, "loo,
　Herken how leccherie dooþ speke !
Whanne þou þi foule luste hast doo,
236　Bi waare him þanne ! he wole þee þrete,
And seie 'for þou hast so doo
　þou must suffre peynes greete ;'
And but if god help þee þo,
240　Soone in wanhope he wole þee lete.

Chastity warns man that Lust when gratified will threaten him with

torments, and he'll fall into despair.

Quod þe good aungil, "ȝit þee avise ;
　Lerne witte while þou art heere ;
He is a foole þat may be wise,
244　In heuene comeþ no foolis to ȝeere,

The Good Angel tells man to consider,

and not be a fool,

[Page 131.]

as God refuses
reckless fools.

God doþ richelees foolis refuse
þat kunnen no good, ne noon wole lere ;
If wordis excuse, werkis accuse,
248   þat makiþ hem worse þan þei were."

At *thirty* years
old, man boasts
of his powers.

"In þritti ȝeer now y abide ;
In discrecioun I haue in-siȝt,
Loueli to goo, and to ride,
252   Ful of manhode & of myȝt."

Conscience re-
proves him for
his vices,

Quod Conscience, "vertues þou puttist aside,
And norischist vicis day & nyȝt."
Quod man in scorn, "lo, Conscience doþ chide!
256   For losse of catel he dar not fiȝt."

and shows him
the cost of Pride,

(as against
Meekness),

"Man, kepe þi richesse," quod Conscience,
"To maynteine pride, it costiþ greete ; '
It costiþ nouȝt, meekenesse ne pacience,
260   But it axiþ greet coost to chide & to beete.

of Lechery,

Gluttony,

Leccherie axiþ greet dispense,
It distroieþ mannis kindeli heete ;
And glotenie coostiþ wiþouten diffence
264   Boþe in diuerse drinkis and meete.

It costiþ greet to use a synne
Envy,

[Page 152.]
þat is clepid foule Enuye,
For it fretiþ man with-inne ;
268   Bodi & soule it doþ distroie.

Sloth,

Slouþis þrifte, it is ful þinne,
It costiþ myche in slouþe to lie ;
Covetousness, and
Avarice.
And Coueitise al þe world wolde wynne,
272   And Auarise aftir more doith crie."

Man justifies
himself.
Youth must do
folly, or Age
would have no
wisdom.

Quod man to Conscience, "ȝouþe axiþ delice ;
For ȝouþe þe course of kinde wole holde ;
But ȝouþe were a foole and nyce,
276   How schulde wijsdom be founde in oolde.

þe corage of ȝouþe, and oolde wise,
Makiþ ȝonge men to be boolde ;
In witt of oolde, worschipe lijs ;
280 In þe witte of wise, kingdom is holde.

Þou wastist þi wynde & spillist þi speche,
þi wordis me is looþ to heere ;
And y dide as þou doist me teche,
284 I schulde neuere make myric chere.
Wenest þou with þin hond heuene to reche ?
þin arme wole not be so longe to ȝcere ;
Now, good Conscience, & þou wolt preche,
288 Goo stele an abite, & bicome a frere."

[Page 133.]

Quod man, y pleie, y wrastile, y sprynge,
þese ioies wolen neuere wende me fro ;
Now alle gamys hom y brynge ;
292 What such as y am, þer ben no moo :
I leepe, y daunce, y skippe, y synge,
I am so myrie y can not seie hoo."
Quod Conscience, " þou schalt weepe & wringe
296 Whanne þei take her leeue to goo."

"Myn iȝen ben cleere & briȝt as glas,
Mi lire as lillye and roose of hewe,
Of schappe & strengþe alle folke y passe,
300 And euere my vertu wexiþ newe."
Quod Conscience, " y loue þee weel þe lasse,
þou usist no werkis of good vertu."
" Goo, Conscience, þou lewide asse,
304 I kepe not þi maneris to sue."

Quod man, " Myne age is fourti ȝeere."
Quod þe world, " y offre to þee my weele."
Quod strengþe, " late no man be þi peere."
308 Quod corage, " late no man with þee deele."

5 *

Right margin glosses:

'I hate to hear you, Conscience, trying to stop my merry-making.

If you will preach, steal a cowl and be a friar.

I play and wrestle,

dance and sing, and never cry Halt ! '
Conscience.
" You'll weep when that's over."

Man.
' My eyes are bright, and I'm stronger than any other man.'

Conscience.
" You do no good works."
Man.
' Conscience, you're an ignorant ass.'

At *forty* years old, man is advised by the World,
Strength,
Courage,

[Page 134.]
Lust,   Quod luste and liking, "make good cheere."
Health,   " I am al hool wiþ þee," quod heele.
Conscience,   Quod Conscience, " wistist þou what þese were?
              312   At nede wole faile þi fleische so freele."

                         Quod Conscience to man in ȝouþe,
                         " Traueile in trouþe in tyme is beste."
and Truth.   Quod trouþe, "gete þee richesse nouþe
Gat riches in'
youth that shall   316   Wherwiþ in oolde to haue þi reste ;
do for age.
                         þouȝ age can as he cowthe,
                         Myȝt & corage he haþ looste,
                         He kepiþ his soule þat kepiþ his mouþe,
              320   For þe soule to þe fleisch is but a goost."

At fifty years old,   "Now am I fifti ȝeere y-wis,
                         Myn heer bigynneþ to change his hewe."
Conscience tells   Quod Conscience, " flee from alle vice,
man to do good
works.   324   And use werkis of good vertu,
                         Late not þi werkis proue þee nyce,
                         Loke þat þou euere be founden trewe."
He prefers   " Fare weel Conscience, weelcome Coueitise !
covetousness.
              328   To be richee now y wole pursue."

[Page 135.]   Quod Conscience, " þat is idil bisynesse,
Conscience dis-
suades him ;   Nedeles richesse to gadre soo ;
Overhope makes
him sin ;   Ouerhope is þe cause y-wisse,
              332   He weneþ ameende al er he goo."
Despair helps too.   Wanhope seiþ, " kepe weel þis,
                         For þe world wole faile us two."
                         Quod Conscience, " chaunge not heuen blis
              336   For helle peyne, sorowe, and woo."

At sixty years   "In sixti ȝeere myn age is piȝte,
old, man
laments his evil   Myn iȝen daswen, myn heer is hoore ;
doings.
                         In my werkis y haue febil in-siȝte,
              340   I fynde no vertu in my stoore.

How schal y reckene with god almy3t?
I am aschamed wondir soore."
Quod Conscience, "certis it were ri3t

How shall he
reckon with God?

" Be holy now or
never."

344   To be holi now or neuere moore."

Quod 3outhe to age, "what doist þou nowþe?
Hange up þin hachet & take þi reste;
þe sunne is past fer bi þe sowthe,

Youth taunts the
old man : he is

past and gone.

348   And hi3eth swiþe in to þe weste."
Quod man, " y serued þee in 3ougþe
And al þe tyme myne cruest leste,
Wiþ sorowe of herte & schrifte of mouþe

[Page 136.]
The old man

repents and will
serve God.

352   To god 3it haue y kepte þe beste."

"Age, calle a3en 3istirday to-morowe;
And alle þi werkis, bigynne hem newe."
Quod man, "þou3 þou speke in scorne,

Youth mocks him
again.

The old man
learns from the
scorn,

356   þou techist me good þat y neuere knewe;
I wole biþinke me on my werkis biforn,
Do almes dede, praie, & rewe,
And goddis mercy schal ynne my corn,

will pray and
sorrow, and God
will in his corn.

360   And fede me wiþ þat þat y neuere sewe.

In 3ougþe whanne y was wilde & stronge,
þe fals world fair dide me wowe,
Me þou3t ech worde a myrie songe,

' When young,
the false world
wooed me,

364   Wiþ pipis, and dauncis, & mirþis y-nowe.
Now seiþ he, he loued me to longe,
For myn heer bigynneþ to blowe;
To þi mercy, lord, me vndirfonge,

but in age has
left me.

Have mercy on
me, Lord.

368   þe tyde is ebbid, & no more wole flowe."

" Þe candel of lijf þi soule dide tende:
To li3te þee hom," resoun dide saye.
" Miche of my candel in waaste y spende,

[Page 137.]
My candle of life
I let winds of
wickedness waste;

372   Manye wickid windis haþ wastid it away;

I can scarcely
hold its end.

Vnneþe y holde my candelis eende,

It is past euensonge of my day ;

To reepe myn heruest, whidir mai y winde ?

376   Mi londis of vertues liggen al lay.

¶ Whanne ȝouþe was maistir, y was page,

I lived in the
Devil's service,
with late suppers
and late rising.

We lyueden myche in þe feendis seruice,

Wiþ rere souperis and wickid outrage,

380   Ligge longe in bed, looþe to arise.

Now the wise
reprove me, and

Now haue y nouȝt but wisschis to wage,

And myche repreef amonge þe wijse ;

former friends
hate me.

þei þat loueden me in ȝouþe, hatiden me in age,

384   And vnkindeli me diden dispice.

I wonder why the
world was made.

NOw haue y greet meruaile

þe world to man whi it was wrouȝte ;

Fele temptaciouns now me assaile,

I have no rest,

388   I haue no reste for chaunge of þouȝte.

[Page 138.]

Whanne y schulde reste y haue greet merueile ;

In bed to sleepe whanne y am brouȝte,

and see nothing
but battle and
dread.

I se but drede and greet bataile

392   Al mannys lijfe, and it be souȝte.

The world has
forsaken me ;

Thus þe fals world haþ forsaken me ;

For waste of hise goodis he accusiþ me ;

my sins accuse
me

þe synnes þat y loued, now haten me,

396   To Conscience þei adwiten me ;

fiends threaten
me ;

Feendis þreten faste to take me,

And steren helle houndis to bite me ;

Death shakes his
spear at me.

Deeþ seiþ, my breed he haþ baken me ;

400   Now schakeþ he his spere to smite me.

I am like a stag
at bay.

Þus y am huntid as an herte to a-bay,

I not whidir y may me turne,

Myne enemyes myȝtili me assay,

404   I waxe feble and vnourne ;

To flee to god is my beste way,

þere schal y in no poynt spurne ;

Lord ! now socour me þat beste may,

408　In þin herte blood, þat holi bourne."

Qnod ȝouþe to age, " y þee forsake,

þi frendis deien, þi strengþe dooþ faile,

þi siȝte and heeryng bigynneþ to slake,

412　þee nediþ helpe and good counsaile ;

God-is seruauntis in arrest haþ þee take

Til deeþ on þee haue doon bataile ;

þi reckenyng bi tyme bisili þou make,

416　Or þe deuel bringe þe countirtaile."

[Page 139.]
Youth taunts Age
with his failing
strength

and Death's ad-
vance on him.
He must make up
his accounts
quickly.

Þouȝ deeþ be eende of worldlis woo,

þanne deeþ is euere mannys freende ;

thouȝ soulis in helle be penischid soo,

420　Deeþ comeþ not þere-to make noon eende ;

Deeþ makiþ soulis to heuen to goo,

But in to heuen deeþ may not wende,

For deeþ is flemyd heuene froo,

424　Deeþ is sugett to god to bende.

To some Death
here is a friend,

but not to any in
hell.

It sends some to
heaven, and there
troubles them not.

"NOw y am sixti ȝeere and ten,

Ȝonge folke Y fynde my foo,

Where euere þei pleie, leepe, or renne,

428　þei þinken in her weie Y goo ;

And whanne y mete with olde men,

I pleyne ' þis world is chaungid soo ;'

Noon oþer bote is but seelde when

432　Ech man telliþ oþir his woo."

At seventy years
old, the man feels
in the way of
young folk ;

[Page 140.]
his only comfort
is in complaints,
and telling other
old men his
troubles.

Quod ȝouþe to age, " y þee a-peele

And þat bifore oure god y-wis ;

I lente þee strengþe, bewte, & heele,—

436　þese percellis ben of heuen blis,—

and wealth
Corage, li3tnesse, freendis, & weele ;
Alle þese þou hast wastide amys

in folly,
From wijsdom in-to folies feele :
440 God wole haue rekenyng of al þis.

his sight in vain-glory, his mouth in oaths and gluttony,
Þine heerynge and þin i3e si3te
þat þou hast wastide in veynglory ;
þi mouþe to wronge a3en ri3te,
444 In fals ooþis and foule gloteny ;

his hands in robbery,
þin hondis to robbe and to fi3te ;
þi strengþe þou wastidist in tyrauntry ;

his beauty in lechery.
þi feet in derknesse oute of li3te,
448 þi bewte þou wastidist in leechery."

[Page 141.] The old man confesses his short-comings,
Quod man, "y was gouerned Bitwene two þeuis,
þei stale on me: Y was stalworþe & white ;
Whanne my leepis weren brou3t to preuis,
452 I wondre on my silf Y was so li3te.

regrets his loss
3ougþe staale from me ; þat soore me greuis ;
Age steeleþ on me boþe day and ny3te ;

of youth and power,
Mi 3ougþe, my vertu, al from me meuis ;
456 Now wondre y on my silf where is my my3te.

and complains how youth, with all its glory, has stolen from him, and age, with all its defects, has stolen upon him.
¶ 3ougþe staale from me, Y was stalworþe & li3te ;
And age steeleþ on me Filþis to weelde ;
3ougþe steeliþ from me, Y 3eede up ri3te ;
460 Age steeleþ on me, Y bowe and 3eelde ;
3ougþe haþ stolen from me My leepis li3te ;
Age steeliþ on me, Y wexe on-mylde ;
3ougþe steeleþ my corage To pleie & fi3te,
464 Age is so on me stoolen þat y mote to god me 3ilde.

At eighty years old
"**N**ow y am euene of 3eeris fore scoure,
So manye wyntir Y am oolde ;
þere y was wonte To leepe bifore,
468 For aboute now My wei y hoolde :

My backe bowiþ, myn iȝen ben soore,

Myn hoote blood is kelid coolde :

Alas ! Conscience ! to litil y toke þi loore,

472 Þe talis þat þou hast ofte me toolde."

[Page 142.]
his back is bent, his hot blood cold. Ah, Conscience ! I did not listen to you.

Quod Conscience, "wherehaddist þou þat speche?

Þi liȝte leepis foonde to preue ;

Þe put of þe stoon þou maist not reche,

476 To litil myȝte is in þi sleue.

In yougþe whanne y dide þee teche,

Foule þou me þanne dedist repreue ;

I þanke god of þi good leeche."

480 "Ȝhe, Conscience, now to þi wordis y leeue."

Conscience wonders at the man's repentance,

but thanks God for it.

"Now foure score ȝeeris is past,

Mi lijf is but traueil & woo,

Fer in to rereage y am cast,

484 Into ten ȝeer and moo.

My lymes foulden þat weren fast,

Wiþ staffe in honde now y goo ;

My redy speche may not last,

488 So my teeþ ben fallen me fro.

At ninety years old man's life is but woe,

he walks with a staff,

his teeth fall out,

Ful of fleissche Y was to fele,

Now may I neiþer stonde ne goon ;

It haþ now lefte me euery dele,

492 Me is lefte But skyn & boon.

Now y am vndre Fortunes whele,

My frendis forsaken me Euerychoon,

And alle þe synnes Y loued so weel,

496 Now wote y weel þei been my foon."

[Page 143.] his flesh is gone,

he is but skin and bone,

forsaken by his friends,

and his sins his foes.

Quod course of kinde, "What helpiþ, y wende,

Þi wissching And þin hadde-y-wist ?

What maist þou On þo wordis spende,

500 It is ful febil In þi fist.

Course of Nature asks the good of his vain regrets.

All men expect
his death, and
none will regret
him; he cumbers
all.

Now alle men waiten aftir þin eende ;

   þou3 þou deye, þou schalt not be myste ;

þou combrest boþe foo & frende,

504   þi mylle haþ grounde þi laste griste."

These mortal
sins must quit the
aged :
Pride,

Pre deedli synnes maden her moone,

"We forsaken man in age."

Quod Pride, "y am from him goon,

508   For Pride in age Doiþ disperage."

Lechery,
[Page 114.]
Gluttony.

Quod leccherie, "He loueþ to lie a-loone ;

þou3 he wolde do, him wantiþ corage."

Quod Glotenie, "he is but felle & boone,

512   He loueþ more mesure þan outrage."

Two think him
no good,
Envy and
Wrath.

Quod Envie, "age hath no my3te

Ne richesse, lenger me to fynde."

Quod wraþþe, "age may not fi3te

516   þou3 he be angri, bi course of kynde."

Two claim him,
Sloth and
Covetousness.

Quod Slouþe, "age my chaumbre haþ di3te,

And calleþ me ease in his mynde."

Quod Coueitise, "age haþ me hi3te ;

520   Suget to me he dooþ him binde."

Overhope, or vain
Confidence that
they will ever do
well, is the cause
of men's waste
and sin.
Then comes
Sickness.

"**I** knowe," quod ouerhope, "fleissch is freele,

Of oolde and 3onge, of man, of childe ;

In ouerhope þei wasten her weele,

524   And in diuerse werkis ful wylde ;

þei ouerhope euere to lyue in heele,

From age & sijknesse þei weneþ hem schilde,

þanne comeþ sijknesse, & printiþ his seele."

Then Wanhope or
Despair,

528   Quod wanhope "þan y make him mylde ;

[Page 145.]
and bids them
hoard.

I bidde him horde, and richesse saue,

For wanhope after mischife doiþ waite,

Whanne sijknesse comeþ men to craue,"

Overhope still
lures them on ;

532   Quod ouerhope, "þan y flatir, & sumtyme flaite,

'þou schalt lyue, and þi silf it haue.' "
" 3he," seiþ wanhope, "kepe it straite,

Despair mocks
them,

Of good hope no councell þou craue
536   Til deep þee caste with a trippe of dissaite."

Quod wanhope, " a gospel y radde :

and tells them the
Gospel; if they

   To telle it þee y wole bigynne,
' If a man in synne be sadde

will plunge daily
into sin, God will
be more pleased
than if they never
sinned.

540   Ech day newe, and lieþ þer-inne,
Of such a man god is moore gladde
þan of a childe þat neuere dide synne."
Quod Conscience, " he wolde make þe madde

Conscience

544   To repente þee not, ne neuere blynne."

Quod Conscience to wanhope, " I-wys

reproves Despair,

   þou liest, y hate þe þerfore ;
I knowe þe gospel, it seiþ þis,

and repeats the
true Gospel, that
of a repentant

548   ' If a man haue synned longe bifore,
And axe mercy And a-mende his mys,

sinner God is
gladder than of
[Page 146.]
one who never
sinned.

   Repente, and wilne to synne no more,
Of þat man god gladder is
552   þan of a child synlees y-bore.' "

Quod wanhope, " a gospel y radde ;

Despair urges
the Gospel that
men suffer as they

   What it meneþ y can expownde,
Ech man schal haue peine or meede,

are found, and as
the old man has
not yet repented, he

556   In þou3te or dede as he is founde ;
He haþ not 3it repentid his dede,
He si3keþ for synnes ben not vnbounde ;
þou3 mercy come, he schal not spede,

cannot get mercy.

560   For in daunger of wanhope he is bounde."

Quod Conscience, " þou dotid hoore !

Conscience says,
' Doted whore,

God-is mercy þou woldist distroie ;
þou wenest þi wickidnesse were moore

God's mercy

564   þan god-is goodnesse & his mercie.

For if a man be woundid soore,

    And axe no medicine, him liste to deie ;

God haþ mercies y-now in stoore

568   For a þousand worldis þat mercie wole crie."

is enough for a
thousand
worlds if they
ask it.'

"**M**Ekenes, Pacience, and Charitee,

    Ȝe þat weren my frendis dere,

Mesure, Bisinesse, and Chastitee,

572   At þis mystire comeþ me neere."

Quod Conscience, " þou flemed us from þee ;

þou woldist not oure loore leere."

Quod richelees, " loo, heere my meynee !

576   þe synnes þat þou louedist & seruedist, lo hem

      here ! "

The *Old Man*
calls on the
Virtues to
befriend

him in his need.

[Page 117.]

Recklessness
offers instead, the
crew of Sins that
he loved.

"**M**yne age is now an hundrid ȝeere ;

    Litil y drinke, and lesse y ete,

On my backe I bere my beere,

580   And alle my frendis me forȝete,

Fayn þei wolde þat y deed were,

Wiþ sorewful wordis þei doon me þretee,

And seyn, ' for y am so longe heere,

584   Whanne y come hoome y schal be beete.'

At a *hundred*
years old man
carries his bier
on his back, all
his friends wish
him dead.

NOw mote y leie forþ my necke,

    For deeþ his swerd out haþ lauȝte ;

But I deliuere weel þis checke,

588   I leese my game at þis drauȝte.

Ful of synne is my secke ;

To þe preest y wole schewe þat frauȝte,

Mi schip is chargid, al gooþ to wrecke

592   But if god of merci be wiþ me sauȝte."

He may stretch
out his neck for
Death's sword ;

he is full of sin ;

he must go to
wreck

unless God have
mercy.

This worlde haþ me in awaite,

    And biddiþ me quite þat is past ;

My fleissche in ouerhope wolde me faite,

596   And into wanhope it wolde me caste.

The World re-
proves him,

Overhope and
Despair tempt
him,

Helle houndis berken and baite,

þe feendis writiþ my synnes faste,

And deeþ me waitiþ with a trippe of dissaite ;

600   These sixe maken me soore agaste."

[Page 148.]
Hell-hounds bark for him, the Fiends and Death watch for him.

Þanne comeþ forþ good hope :

    To saue man he wolde fonde ;

"þou wronge weuere ouerhope !

604   I make him free, þou woldist make him bonde ;

I schal conclude þee, þou wanhope,

    Wile good feiþ wole with me stoonde ;

Hooli writte seiþ, ' in god y hoope,

608   His merci is ouer þe werkis of his honde."

But *Good Hope* will save the old man,

if Good Faith will help.

Quod good feiþ, " for þe litil while

    þat now heere [þou] hast serued me,

I wole þee kepe from al perile,

612   And make pees bitwene god & þee ;

And ouerhope, for al his gile,

    From þin herte y schal do him flee ;

And wanhope also y wole exile,

616   For he is not of oure fraternitee."

Good Faith will

make his peace with God,

and drive out

Overhope and Despair.

Quod þe worlde, Y wole hise dettis quyte,

    And oute of his daunger me hyȝe ;

þouȝ my fleissche berke, he schal not bitee,

620   From his lustis y wole him tye ;

I wole waissche a-'Wey þat feendis write

    With sorowe of herte and teer of yȝe,

But with deeþ y wole not dispuite,

624   But make me cleene, and leerne to deie.

Man says he will

give up his fleshly

[1 Page 149.]
lusts, will sorrow and weep,

and learn to die.

God ! sowe þi merci amonge my seede,

þanne schal it growe þouȝ y sowe late,

And Repentaunce my corne schal weede,

628   And make good pees þere was hate.

May God sow His mercy in him, and Repentance will weed his corn.

þe comaundementis þat god bede,
þat is þe locke of heuen ȝate ;

Then the works
of Mercy will let
him in at heaven's
gate.

Seuene werkis of mercy, and þe crede,

632   þese keies schullen late me in þerate."

Reader, you have
heard of Youth
and Age, Virtue
and Vice, Good
Angel and Bad.

Now haue ȝe herde of ȝouþis delice ;
And age in kynde, sijke, & woo ;
Knowing of uertu & of vice ;

636   Good aungil, & wickid freende, & foo ;
And vndirstondinge to be wijs.

Look in this
Mirror; take
your choice, for
Heaven or Hell.

Now in þis mirrour loke ȝou soo ;
In ȝoure free wille þe choice lijs,

640   To heuen or helle whiþir ȝe wille goo.

The world, the
flesh, and the
devil tempt us.

The worlde, þe fleiȝsche, & þe feende,
In temptacioun doiþ us chase ;
Bid repentaunce to merci beende,

644   And waissche us at þe welle of grace.

[Page 150.]
Let us pray to
God

that after death
we may see His
fair face.

Praie we to god graunte us good eende,
And in heuen to haue a place,
þat after oure deeþ we mowen þidir wende,

648   And in perfiȝt loue se his fair face.

Dear friends, who
read this, pray
for the Writer's
soul to Mary,
Mother,

Now, leeue freendis, greete and smale,
þat haue herde þis trete,
Praie for þe soule þat wroot þis tale

652   A Pater noster, & an aue
To marie modir, maiden free,
As sche bare a childe Coumforte to us,
On þat soule haue pitee

to pity it if
Christ will.
Amen.

656   If þe wille be of crist ihesus.   **amen.**

[*Stans Puer*, printed in *Babees Boke, &c.*, p. 27, follows here.]

God send us Paciens in oure Oolde Age!

[*Pages* 113—17, *written without breaks.*]

FRom þe tyme þat we were born
   oure ȝouþe passiþ from day to day,
And age encreesiþ moore & moore,
4   & so doiþ it now, þe sothe to say :
At euery hour a poynt is y-loore,
   So fast gooþ oure ȝouþe away,
And ȝouþe wole come aȝen no moore,
8   But age wole make us boþe blak & gray.
þerfore take hede boþe nyȝt & day
   How fast ȝoure ȝouþe dooþ asswage ;
And boþe ȝonge & oolde, lete us praie
12   þat god send us paciens in oure oolde age.

¶ Age wole take from us oure myȝt
   þat in oure ȝouþe to us was lent ;
And also þe cleernesse of oure syght
16   And oure heerynge schal be faynt.
þanne schulen we be heuy þat eer were liȝt,
   Bicause þat ȝouþe is from us went,
And þanne wole men do us no riȝt,
20   But al contrarie to oure entent,
And sikenes wole do us greet turment
   Whom deeþ wole sende on his message ;
Forsoþe þe best ameendement
24   is þanne pacience in oure olde age.

Our youth passes away from day to day,

and will come back no more,

Take heed, then,

and pray God for patience in old age.

Age will take from us

our clear sight, hearing,

and lightness.

Sickness will torment us.

[Page 114.]

Our bones will
ache,

Oure body wole icche, *oure* bonis wole ake,
　　oure owne fleisch wole ben *oure* foo ;

our head shake,

Oure heed, *oure* hondis, þo wolen schake,
28　　And oure leggis wole tremble where we go ;
Oure bonis wole drie as dooþ a stake,
　　And in *oure* bodi we schulen be woo,

our nose turn
black,

Oure nose, *oure* chekis, wolen wexe al blake,
32　　& oure glad chere wole fade us fro ;
And whanne oure teeþ ben goon also,

our tongue lose
its fair speech.

　　Oure tunge schal lese his fair langage :
Praie we for us silf & oþer moo
36　　þat god sende us paciens in *oure* olde age !

Our friends will
hate us ;

Oure freendis þat schulden loue us best,
　　þanne wole þei haue us but in hate,
In freendschip is þer noon oþer trust,
40　　& þerof be we waare to late.

we shall say, 'Oh,
if I had but
known ; '
no kiss will
greet us

þan may we synge of had y wist,
　　Oure feynt freendis han us forsake,
And also we schulen go vnkist
44　　boþe at þe dore & at þe gate ;

and no joy
gladden us.
[1 Page 115.)
God send us
patience in our
old age !

And for al þe cheer þat we can make,
　　þan is [1] no ioie of *oure* visage :
Whanne *oure* bewte schal aslake,
48　　god send us paciens in *oure* olde age !

¶ we schulen be so angri euermore,
　　we wolden ben awreke of euery wrong,
þanne summe wolen scorne us þerfore,

Some will scorn
us, others think
we live too long ;

52　　& summe wole seie we lyue to long ;
Oure sorowe wole þan sitte us so soore

our stomachs will
take no food ;

　　Oure stomak wole no mete fonge ;
& eueri day more & more

we shall sing of
sorrow and care.

56　　Of sorewe & care schal be *oure* song.
whanne we were boþe hool & strong
　　we were to wie[l]de, & wold out rage,

And þerfore lete us praie among

60   þat god send us paciens *in* oure olde age.

¶ For þan wole no þing us availe

        but *oure* bedis and oure crucche,

for wordli welþe wole fade & faile,

64   And *þerfore* truste we it not to myche ;

        & þan wole sijknes us assaile

        Til it haþ made us lijk a wrecche,

        & þan may we do no greet traueile

68   But ¹summtyme grone, & sumtyme grucche,

And sumtyme clawe for scabbe & icche

        Whanne age haþ us at his auauntage :

        Who-so lyueþ long schal be such ;

72   God sende us paciens *in* oure olde age !

¶ Al þat we haue lyued heere,

        It is but as a dreem y-met,

For now it is as it neuere were,

76   And so is it þat is to comyng ȝit.

Ful fast we drawen to *oure* beere,

        In sorewe & drede we schulen be sett.

Of oolde men þe ȝonge may lere,

80   And fewe þer ben þat doon þe bett ;

For þe feend haþ cauȝt hem in his nett,

        And holdiþ hem fast in bondage

For þei schulden not dispose her witt

84   To haue pacience in her oolde age.

¶ þanne schulen we se þat worldli blis

        Is but a þing of vanite,

        And it makiþ men to do amys

88   þat ben in weelþe & greet bewte ;

And þerfor, lord, good riȝt it is

        With *oure* owne staf chastisid to be :

Lord ! ȝeue us *grace* to þinke on þis,

92   As þou bouȝt us alle upon a tree,

And þat we may in charite

Weel passe ou*er* þis passage

In-to þe blis þat euer*e* schal be,

96   Whanne we be*n* passid *oure* oolde age.

["Bothe ʒonge & olde," or "Se what oure lord suffride for
oure sake," printed above, pp. 32-4, follows here.]

This World is but a Vanyte.

AN OLD MAN'S LAMENT.

[*Lambeth MS. 853, ab. 1430, A.D., page 58 ;
written without breaks.*]

AS Y GAN wandre in my walkinge
 Bisidis an holt vndir an hille,
Y say an oolde man sitte wepinge :
4 With siȝynge sore he seide me tille,
 ¶ "Sumtime y hadde þe world at wille,
  With ricchesse & with rialte,
 And now it is turned al to ille ;
8 þe worlde is but a vanyte.

In my walk

*I saw an old man
sighing, and he
said, " Once I
had all the world
at my will, but
now it's all
turned to ill.*

My silf I likne vnto þe morewe :
 Whanne y was child, & bor[e]n bare,
Mi modir for me suffride sorewe
12 With gruntyngis gril & siȝinge sare;
 ¶ On me was neiþer wem ne hore ;
  But siþen in synne y haue be ;
 Now y am oolde y wepe þerfore ;
16 þis world is but a vanyte.

*I am like the
Morning. At my
birth my Mother
groaned with
pain.*

I was spotless,

*but now am
sinful.*

 At mydmore y lerned to go,
 And plaied as children doon in ¹strete ;
þe kinde of childhode y dide also,
20 Wiþ my felawis to fiȝte and þrete.
 ¶ Al þat y dide, it þouȝte me swete,
  For al þis childhode tauȝte me ;
 Now y am oolde, þerfore y wepe ;
24 þis worlde is but a vanite.

*At Mid-morn I
played,
 [¹ Page 59.]
and like a boy
fought.*

*All I did, seemed
sweet : but now I
weep for it.
This world is but
vanity.*

6 *

At Undern
9 A.M.) I was put
to school,

At vndre*n* to scole y was sett
   To lerne lore, as o*þ*ir doo*þ* ;
Whan*n*e my maistir wolde me bet,

and cursed my
master when he
beat me.
28   I wolde him curse, y was ful wrou*þ*.

I cared only for
joy and jollity,
¶ To lerne good y was ful loo*þ*,
   I *þ*ou*ʒ*te on ioie & ioilite ;
Now certis, for to seie *þ*e soo*þ*,

alas!
32   *þ*is world is b*u*t a vanyte.

At Mid-day I was
knighted,

At mydday y was dubbid kny*ʒ*t,
   In route y lerned for to ryde ;
Was *þ*er noon so hardi a wi*ʒ*t

and none durst
stand my charge.
36   *þ*at in bataile durste me abide.

Where is now my
bravery ? Not to
be hidden from
death.
¶ Where is bicome now al my pride,
   Mi booldnes, & my fair bewte ?
Now from dee*þ* may y me not hide ;

40   *þ*is world is b*u*t a vanyte.

At High Noon I
was crowned
King, and fulfil-
led all my lusts.
[¹ Page 60.]

At hi*ʒ* noo*n* y was crowned king,
   *þ*is world was oonli at my wille ;
Euer*e* to ¹ lyue was my liking,

44   And alle my lustis to fulfille.

Now age has
crept on me.
¶ Now age is cropen on me ful stille,
   And maki*þ* me oold & blac of ble,
And y go downeward wi*þ* *þ*e hille ;

This world is but
vanity.
48   *þ*is World is but a vanite.

At Mid-afternoon
my pleasures
passed away.

At mydoue*r*noon y droupid faste,
   Mi lust & liking wente away ;
From iolite myn hert is paste,

52   From rialte & riche aray.

Man's life here is
but a day com-
pared to everlast-
ing life.
¶ Man*n*is lijf here is but a day
   A*ʒ*ens *þ*e lijf *þ*at euer*e* schal be ;
And oo *þ*ing y dare weel say,

56   *þ*at *þ*is world is but a vanyte.

At euensong tyme y wax ful coold,
   And bigan to go bi staue ;
Now is deeþ on me ful boold,
60   And for his rent he wole me craue.
  ¶ Whanne y am deed & leid in graue,
    þer is no þing þanne þat saueþ me
  But good or yuel þat y do haue ;
64   þis world is but a vanite.

At Even Song I walked with a staff. Death seeks me.

In the grave nought saues but good done.

Thus is þe day come to nyȝt,
   þat me loþith of my lyuynge,
And doolful deeþ to me is diȝt,
68   And in coold ¹clay now schal y clinge."
  ¶ þus an oold man y herde mornynge
    Biside an holte vndir a tree.
  God graunte us his blis euerlastinge !
72   þis world is but a vanite.

At Night I loathe my life. Death and the Grave possess me.

[¹ Page 61.]

God grant us His bliss ! for this world is but vanity.

[" In a noon tijd," or " Reuertere," pp. 91-4 of this volume,
follows here in the MS.]

This World is False and Vain.

[Lambeth MS. 853, page 32, written without breaks.]

Whi is þis world biloued þat fals is & veyn,
Siþen þat hise welþis ben so unserteyn ?

¶ Al so soone hee passiþ his power away
4 As dooþ a brokil poot þat freisch is and gay.

¶ Truste ȝe raþer to lettris written wiþinne þis
þan to þis wrecchid world þat ful of synne is.

¶ It is fals in his biheeste, & riȝt disceyuable ;
8 It haþ bigilid many a man, it is so vnstable.

¶ It is raþir ¹ to bileeue þe wageringe wijnde
þan þe chaungeable world þat makiþ men so blinde.

¶ For wheþer þou slepe or wake, þou schalt fynde it fals
12 Bothe in hise bisinessis & in hise lustis als.

¶ Telle me where is Salamon, sumtyme a king richee,

Or Sampson þe stronge to whom was no man liche ?

¶ Or þe fair man absolon, merueilose in cheere,

16 Or þe duke ionatas, a weel biloued fere ?

¶ Where is bicome cesar, þat lorde was of al,

Or þe riche man clopid in purpur & in pal ?

¶ Telle me where ys tullius, in eloquence so sweete,

20 Or aristotil þe Filosofre wiþ his witt so greete ?

¶ Where ben þese worþi þat were heere-to-forn ? *or all former*
Boþe kingis & bischopis, her power is al lorn. *kings ? All their power is lost,*

¶ Alle þese greete princis with her power so hiȝe *all vanished in the twinkling of an eye.*
24 Ben vanischid now a-way in twynkeling[1] of an yȝe. *[1 Page 34.]*

¶ þe ioie of þis wreechid world is a schoorte feeste, *This world's joy is a passing shadow,*
And it is likened to a schadewe þat may not longe leste,

¶ And ȝit it drawiþ man from heuen riche blis, *and yet makes man lose heaven.*
28 And ofte tyme it makiþ him to synne & do a-mys.

¶ Calle no þing þine owne, þerfore, þat þou maist *Call nothing here thine own ;*
heere leese ;
For þat þe world haþ lent þee, efte he wole it cese.

¶ Sette þin herte in heuene a-boue, & þenke what *set thy heart on heaven above.*
ioie is þere,
32 And þus to dispise þe world y rede þat þou lere.

¶ þou þat art but wormes meete, poudre, & dust, *Thou food for worms, exalt not thyself in pride ;*
To enhaunce þi silfe in pride sett not þi lust.

¶ For þou woost not to-day þat þou schalt lyue to- *thou may'st die to-morrow.*
morowe,
36 þerfore do þou euere weel, And þanne schalt þou *Therefore do well.*
not sorowe.

¶ It were ful ioieful & sweete, lordschipe to haue, *Lordship would be good if it could save a man,*
If so þat lordschip miȝte a man fro [2]deeþ saue, *[2 Page 35.]*

¶ But for as myche as a man schal deie at þe laste, *but it is no honour, only a burden.*
40 It is noo worschip, but a charge, lordschip to
taaste.

Omnia terrena *All earthly things are another's by turns,*
Per vices sunt aliena :
nescio sunt cuius ; *now mine, now another's.*
44 mea nunc, cras huius et huius.
Dic, homo, quid speres, *What do you hope for, if you cleave wholly to this world ?*
si mundo totus adheres ;
nulla tecum feres, *You can take nothing out of it but yourself.*
48 licet tu solus haberes.

Earth.

Whanne liif is moost loued, and deeþ is moost hatid :
þanne dooþ deeþ drawe his drawȝt, and makiþ man
ful nakid.

De terra plasmasti me, &c.

Man, made of
earth, has only

cared how he may
be set high up on
earth.

ERþe out of erþe is wondirly wrouȝt,
Erþe of erþe haþ gete a dignyte of nouȝt,
Erþe upon erþe haþ sett al his þouȝt,
4 How þat erþe upon erþe may be hiȝ brouȝt.

Man would be a
king on earth ;
but when earth
[¹ Page 36.]
bids him home,
he shall find it
hard to part.

¶ Erþe upon erþe wold be a king ;
But how erþe schal to erþe, þenkiþ he no ¹ þing ;
Whanne þat erþe biddiþ erþe hise rentis hom
    bring,
8 þan schal erþe out of erþe haue a piteuous parting.

Man wins on
earth castles, and
says ' It is ours.'

But he shall
suffer sharply for
it.

¶ Erþe vpon erþe wynneþ castels & touris,
þan seiþ erþe to erþe ' now is þis al houris :'
Whanne erþe upon erþe haþ biggid up hise
    boure[s],
12 þanne schal erþe upon erþe suffir scharpe schouris.

Man goes on earth

glittering in gold,
and yet he shall
return to earth
before he likes.

¶ Erþe gooþ vpon erþe as molde upon molde,
So gooþ erþe upon erþe al gliteringe in golde,
Like as erþe vnto erþe neuere go schulde ;
16 And ȝit schal erþe vn-to erþe raþer þan he wolde.

Wretched man,
who toilest

¶ O þou wrecchid erþe þat on erþe traueilist nyȝt
    and day

To florische þe erþe, to peynte þe erþe *with* wan- *to adorn thee with fine raiment,*
    towne aray ;

ȝit schal þou, erþe, for al þi erþe, make þou it *yet shalt thou*
    neuere so queynte & gay,

20 Out of þis erþe into þe erþe, þere to clinge as a *return to earth like a clod.*
    clot of clay.

¶ O wrecchid man, whi art þou proud [1] þat art of *[1 Page 37.]*
    þe erþe makid ? *Why art thou proud who art made of earth ?*

Hider brouȝttist þou no schroud, But poore come *Thou camest to earth naked, and*
    þou, and nakid ;

Whanne þi soule is went out, & þi bodi in erþe *when thou art put in earth, all*
    rakid,

24 þan þi bodi þat was rank & Vndeuout, Of alle *men will hate thee.*
    men is bihatid.

¶ Out of þis erþe cam to þis erþe þis wrecchid *Thy clothing came from earth*
    garnement ;

To hide þis erþe, to happe þis erþe, to *him* was *to enwrap thy earth,*
    cloþinge lente ;

Now gooþ erþe upon erþe, ruli, raggid, and rent, *which under the*
28 þerfore schal erþe vndir þe erþe haue hidiose *earth shall have torment.*
    turment.

¶ Whi þat erþe to myche loueþ erþe, wondir me *Why earth(man) loves earth too*
    þink, *much, I wonder,*

Or whi þat erþe for super*flue* erþe to sore sweete
    wole or swynk ;

For whanne þat erþe upo*n* erþe is brouȝt *with*- *for when man comes to the*
    i*n*ne þe brink, *grave's brink he shall have a sad*

32 þan schal erþe of þe erþe haue a rewful swynk. *time of it.*

¶ Lo, erþe upon erþe, considere þou may *Man, thou camest into earth naked,*
    How erþe comeþ i*n*to erþe nakid al way,

¶ Whi schulde erþe upon erþe go now so stoute or *[Page 38.]*
    gay

and shall be so
when thou diest.

36   Whanne erþe schal passe out of erþe in so poore
           aray ?

Think on this, and
of the judgment
at thy resurrec-
tion,

¶ Wolde god, þerfore, þis erþe, While þat he is
           upon þis erþe, Vpon þis wolde hertile þinke,
   And how þe erþe out of þe erthe schal haue his
           aȝen-risynge,
   And þis erþe for þis erþe schal ȝeelde streite
           rekenyng ;

and then never
for this earth
shalt thou dis-
please God.

40   Schulde neuere þan þis erþe for þis erþe mysplese
           heuene king.

Pray therefore,

¶ þerfore, þou erþe, vpon erþe þat so wickidli hast
           wrouȝt,
   While þat þou, erþe, art upon erþe, turne aȝen þi
           þouȝt,

man, to God,

   And praie to þat god upon erþe þat al þe erþe
           haþ wrouȝt,

that thou may'st
come to bliss.

44   þat þou, erþe upon erþe, to blis may be brouȝt.

Lord, let not man
come to grief for
this earth, but

¶ O þou lord þat madist þis erþe for þis erþe, &
           suffridist heere peynes ille,
   Lete neuere þis erþe for þis erþe myscheue ne
           spille,

[¹ Page 38.]
here ever work
thy will, that he
may ascend to
thy high hill.

   But þat þis erþe on þis ¹erþe be euere worchinge
           þi wille,
48   So þat þis erþe from þis erþe may stie up to þin
           hiȝ hille.   A-M-E-N.

[See an earlier Poem on *Earth*, in alternate English and Latin
stanzas, in my edition of *Early English Poems* for the Philological
Society, 1862, p. 150-2; and in *Reliquiæ Antiquæ*, vol. ii. p. 216.
    Memento homo quod cinis es, and the Creed (pp. 101-3 of this
Text), follow here in the MS.

Reuertere!

(IN ENGLISCH TUNGE, TURNE AȜEN!)

[*Lambeth MS.* 853, *ab.* 1430 A.D., *page* 61, *written without breaks.*]

IN a noon tijd of a somers day
    þe sunne schoon ful myrie þat tide,
I took myn hauk al for to play,
4   Mi spaynel rennyng bi my side.
¶ A feisaunt hen soone gan y se,
    Myn hound put up ful fair to fliȝt,
I sente my faukun, y leet him flee:
8   It was to me a deinteuose siȝt.

¶ My faukun fliȝ faste to his pray,
    I ran þo with a ful glad chere,
I spurned ful soone on my way,
12   Mi leg was hent al with a brere.
¶ þis brere forsoþe dide me grijf,
    And soone it made me to turne aȝe,
For he bare written in euery leef
16   þis word in latyn, reuertere.

I knelid & pullid þe brere me fro,
    And redde þis word ful hendeli;
Myn herte fil doun vnto my too
20   þat was woont sitten ful likingly.
¶ I leete myn hauke & feysaunt fare,
    Mi spaynel fil doun to my knee,

One sunny summer noon I took out my hawk and spaniel.

The dog put up a hen pheasant, and I flew my falcon at her—a pretty sight.

I ran on fast,

but a briar brought me to grief, and made me turn back, for on every leaf it was written *Reuertere*.

I disentangled myself.

My heart fell to my toe.
[Page 62.]

I let the hawk and hen fly,

and sighed over
this *Reuertere*.

þanne took y me wiþ siȝynge sare

24　　þis new lessoun, reuertere.

It means 'turn
again, or back.'

Reuertere is as myche to say

In englisch tunge as, turne aȝen :

Turn, then, man
and think of thy
life, open and
hidden.

Turne aȝen, man, y þee pray,

28　　And þinke hertili what þou hast ben ;

¶ Of þi liuynge be-þinke þee rijfe,

In open & in priuite.

If thou would'st
go to heaven,
think of '*turn
again*.'

þat þou may come to euerlastinge lijf,

32　　Take to þi mynde reuertere.

I became serious,

Þis word made me to studie sore,

And binam me al my list ;

and thought how
I had spent my
life.

How y hadde ledde my lijf so ȝore,

36　　I putt it freischli in-to my brist.

I found myself
full far from God,

¶ þanne foond y me ful fer y-flet

Al from god in maieste ;

Forsoþe þere schal no þing me leett

and will repent.

40　　þat y ne wole synge reuertere.

This summer-
noon heat

[¹ Page 63.]

This noon hete of þe someris day,

Whanne þe sunne moost ¹ hiȝest is,

is like

It may be likened in good fay,

44　　For gregorie witnessiþ weel þis ;

man in youth,
rushing into all
kinds of sin.

¶ For in ȝonge age men wide doon walke

To dyuers synnis in fele degre :

þouȝ a ȝong man make a balke,

48　　Ȝit take to þi mynde reuertere.

Lust blinds many
a man,

For likinge blindiþ many oon

þat he seeþ not him-silf y-wis,

And makiþ his herte as hard as stoon ;

and prevents him
thinking of
heaven.

52　　þanne þenkiþ he not on heuen blis ;

¶ For danyel preueþ it weel riȝtfulli,

As susannis storie telliþ me,

Two preestis were deemed worþili ;
56   For likinge þei know not reuertere.

3ouþe beriþ þe hauke upon his hond
    Whanne ioilite for3etiþ age :
This hauke is mannis herte, y vndirstonde,
60   For it is 3ong & of hi3 romage.
¶ He puttiþ his hauke fro his fist,
    He þat schulde to god be free ;
He meltiþ and wexiþ a weel poore gist
64   Whanne 'he comeþ to reuertere.

Youth bears the hawk on his hand.

The hawk is man's heart, and

is flown from the fist, but not to God.

[¹ Page 64.]

For ful of corage is 3ougeþe in herte,
    And waity3nge euere on his pray,
He ne spariþ ryuer ne þornes smerte
68   To gete his myrþe þere he beest may.
¶ He þat enserchiþ þe derknes of ny3t,
    And þe myst of þe morowtide may se,
He schal know bi cristis my3t
72   If 3ouþe kunne synge reuertere.

Youth watches ever its prey, and

spares no prick of thorn to get its pleasure.

Let the watcher of the night ask whether youth will heed the call ' *Turn again.*'

This hauk of herte in 3ouþe y-wys,
    Pursueþ euere þis feisaunt hen ;
þis feisaunt hen is likingnes,
76   And euere folewiþ hir þese 3onge men.
¶ þis is likinge in euery synne,
    Venial & deedli wheþer it be,
With greet likinge he wole bigynne,
80   But sorewe bringe forþ reuertere.

This hawk, man's heart, pursues ever the hen pheasant Pleasure.

Lust or Desire is the beginning of every sin,

Liking is modir of synnis alle,
    And norischiþ euery wickid dede,
In feele myscheues sche makiþ to falle,
84   Of al sorowe sche dooþ þe daunce leede.
¶ þis herte of 3ouþe is hic ¹ of port,
    And wildenes makiþ him ofte to fle,

their mother, and nourisher,

and of all sorrow leads the dance.

[¹ MS. his.]
[Page 65.]
Youth, through wildness,

often goes wrong.
Then it should
turn again.

And ofte to falle in wickid sort ;

88   þanne is it þe beste, reuertere.

But be waar of welþe or þou be woo ;

In iolite whan þou art piȝt,

þinke þat ȝonge wole go þe fro,

92   Be þou neuere so greet of miȝt.

Whanne age haþ take þee bi þe brest,

And for febilnes þou myȝt not se,

þin herte seiþ þanne þat it is best

96   For to seie & synge reuertere.

In pleasure,
think that youth
must leave thee.

When age takes
thee, thou wilt
think it best to
turn again.

Holy Writ says
that a request too
long delayed will
be refused.

But in holi writt we fynde

If þou þi lord schulde ouȝt aske a þing,

For þi longe beinge bihinde,

100   Aȝenseid art þou of þin askinge.

¶ While þou were ȝonge, in tendre age,

Of þin askinge þou were ful free

In ydilnes & wilde outrage ;

104   þanne was forȝete reuertere.

In youth thou
didst wild out-
rage and forgat-
test *Revertere.*

Let every one
think how short a
time he shall be
here.

Þerfore euery man biþinke him weel

How litil while is his dwellynge ;

As holy writt yt dooþ telle,

108   He schal not ¹ knowe with-oute lesinge.

¶ A cok can crowe his tyme mydnyȝt,

Which he knowith weel in his degre :

But his tyme he knowith not ariȝt

112   þat can weel neuere seie reuertere.

[¹ Page 66.]

Cocks crow when
midnight comes.
Man knows not his
time if he cannot
say *Revertere.*

Think, then, man,
that there is no
so poor wretch as
thou.

Therfore be þou in certein, man,

While þou muste knowe how ;

Biþinke þi silf how þou art þan ;

116   Noon so poore a wrecche as þou !

¶ þerfore praye we to heuene king,

Euery man in his degree,

To graunte them þe blis euerlastinge

120   þat þis word weel kan seie, reuertere.

Pray we all to
God to grant over-
lasting bliss to all
who can say
'*Turn again.*'

Merci Passiþ Riȝtwisnes.

(A DIALOGUE BETWEEN A SINNER AND MERCY.)

[*Lambeth MS.* 853, *ab.* 1430 A.D., *pages* 66 *to* 73; *written without breaks.*]

BI a forest as y gan walke
    With-out a paleys in a leye,
I herde two men togidre talke;
4   I þouȝte to write what þei wolde seie.
    ¶ þat oon stood in a doolful aray,
        Hise deedli synnis he gan to defie,
    "Alas," he seide, me dreediþ to-day
8   þat riȝt wole forþ, & no mercye."

    ¶ þanne answeride merci with sobir [1]cheer,
    "Man, me þinkiþ þi witt is bare;
If þou wolt, y schal þee leer,
12   þee nediþ not to moorne so sare.
    ¶ I rede þee to foonde to ameende þi fare;
        Go euery day & heere a messe,
And schryue þee cleene, & haue noo care,
16   For mercy passiþ riȝtwisnes."

    ¶ þanne seide þe synner with angri mood,
    "Man, me þenkist[2] þou doest raue;
I woot weel þou canst no good,
20   þou barist neuere staat but as a knawe.

As I walked I heard two men talking.

One was very sad, fearing that Right would be done, without Mercy.

[1 Page 67.] But *Mercy* said, Man, you

need not mourn.

Amend your ways, hear Mass daily, be shriven, and fear not, Mercy passeth Righteousness.

The *Sinner* answered, Thou ravest:
[2 *for* þenkiþ]

¶ As y deserue, so schal y haue ;
　　Weel bittirli y schal a-bic ;
　I knowe noon helpe þat me schulde haue,

24　　But þat riȝt schal forþ, and no mercie."

¶ þanne seide mercye meeke & mylde,
　　" If þou wolt fro þi synnes drawe,
　þouȝ þou speke þese wordis wilde,
28　　To helpe þee ȝit I wolde be fawe.

¶ Loue weel god, þat is my sawe,
　　Repente þee blyue of ¹ al þi mys ;
　Almyȝti god is ouer þe lawe,
32　　His merci passiþ his riȝtwisnes."

" Seie me," quod þe synner, " þou fonoued ² clerk.
　　þou coudist neuere rede in no spel ;
　I wrouȝte wilfulli neuere good werk ;

36　　What riȝt haue y in heuen to dwelle ?

¶ I haue deserued to go to helle,
　　And þerfore ofte sore sike y ;

　My wickid dedis wole me quelle,
40　　þere riȝt schal forþ, and no mercye."

¶ Merci seide " þou canst no good ;
　　God schewiþ þee kyndenes many foolde,
　For þee & me he schedde his blood,
44　　And suffride woundis bittir & colde.

¶ His fair body to þe iewis was solde
　　To bie oure synful soulis to blis ;

　þi soule is his, y myȝt be bolde ;
48　　His merci passiþ his ryȝtwisnes."

¶ " Forsoþe," quod þe synner, " þat leue y weel,
　　þat he is boþe good & kynde,
　And þerto trewer þan ony steel ;
52　　þat he loueþ truþe weel schal y fynde.

¶ How myȝt god me of care vnbinde
   Siþen god loueþ trouþe so verrili?
Do way, mercy, þou spillist myche winde,
56   For riȝt schal forþ, & no mercy."

[Page 69.]
How then shall
He free me?

Right will pre-
vail, not Mercy.

¶ Merci seide, " woldist þou god knowe,
   And wiþ good entent mercy calle,
And to him meekeli þee abowe,
60   þan schal neuere myscheef in þee falle.
¶ þouȝ þou haddist do þe synnis alle,
   And þou crie mercy for al þi mys,
And with good herte on him to calle,
64   þan wole his mercy passe riȝtwisnes."

Mercy.

If thou wilt really
pray for mercy,

though thou hast
sinned all the
sins,

God's Mercy will
exceed His
Justice.

¶ " What," quod þe synner, " y trowe þou raue ;
   Canst þou neuere of þi pletinge blynne?
þe deuel bad me neuere mercy craue,
68   And he can more clergie þan al þi kynne ;
¶ And he him silf is ful of synne,
   And ȝit wole he neuere mercy crie :
I coueite neuere heuen to wynne
72   While riȝt schal forþ, & no mercie."

The Sinner.

Nonsense! The
Devil bad me
never ask mercy;
and he knows
more than thou.

He is full of sin,
and never asks
mercy;

Justice will
prevail.

¶ Merci seide " y preue bi skile,
   Witt is nouȝt worþ, but grace be souȝt ;
þe deuel ¹Haþ clergie & witt at wille,
76   And euere he settiþ it foule at nouȝt :
¶ He fil in wanhope as him neuere rouȝte,
   þoruȝ pride in heuen he loste his blis ;
Hadde he oonys grace bisouȝte,
80   Merci hadde passid riȝtwijsnes."

Mercy.

The devil's wit is
no good without
grace.
[¹ Page 70.]

He fell into de-
spair when he
lost heaven.
Had he sought
grace he'd have
had Mercy.

¶ Whanne þe synner herd þis, he siȝed sore,
   With rewful cheer greet dool he made,
And seide, " of þee wole y lerne more ;
84   þan is the deuel fals and bad,
¶ For if he myȝte merci haue had,

The Sinner.

I'll learn of thee.
The devil must be
bad if he might
have had mercy.

He needs be sorry who gets Right and not Mercy.
MS. *transposes* riƷtwisnes *and* mercy.]

A þousand siþis y him defie ;
He may be sory & no-þing glad
88   þat schal haue ¹riƷtwisnes & no mercy."

Mercy.

Dear brother, give up the devil, who would send you to hell.

Mercy biheeld þat semeli goost,
And seide, " leue broþer, forsake þe feend,
For he wolde fayn þi soule were lost,
92   To dwelle in helle wiþout eend.

Pray for grace, God will send it, and thy soul will go to heaven.

¶ Biseche now grace, & god wole sende
And þou wolt do as y þee wijs,
And þan þi soule to heuen schal wende,
96   þere merci passiþ riƷtwisnes."

The Sinner.
[Page 71.]
My past life is worthless; I will serve God ; may He keep me from sin.

" Alas," quod þe synner, " al my lijf y rue,
For it is no þing as y wende ;
To serue god y wole be trewe
100   If ony grace he wole me sende.

I defy the false fiend who promised me Right, not Mercy.

¶ Of al wickidnes he me defende !
þe fals feend, y him defie ;
He wolde no þing þat y dide meende,
104   þat biheet me riƷt & no mercie."

Mercy.

Do so, and rejoice. Be sorry for thy sin, be shriven, do

Merci seide " if þou wolt so,
þou myƷt be glad al þi lijf,
And for þi synne þou maist be woo,
108   And to a preest cleene þee schriue,

penance, and

¶ And take penaunce wiþout strijf,

repent : Thou shalt know that Mercy passes Justice.

Repentynge þee of al þi mys,
þan bi þi witt þou maist knowe rijf
112   þat merci passiþ riƷtwisnes."

The Sinner.

No penance is enough for me : not being buried alive.

" Alas," quod the synner, y haue lyued wrong !
What penaunce were y worþi to haue ?
þer may no man sette me to strong
116   þouƷ y were quicke doluen on graue.

¶ A ! almiƷty god, mercy I craue,
  Now leto my flesche my synnis abie !
Graciose crist ! my soule þou haue,
120   For riƷt is nouƷt wiþout mercie."

Mercy seide, " ful weel þou woost,
  As þou hast often herd sayen,
What man is founde þat was lost,
124   Wiþ him is crist plesid & fayn.
¶ What nede had crist to suffre payne
  But for to bie oure soulis to blis ?
Telle me þi lijf heere al playn,
128   þat mercy may passe riƷtwisnes."

" **M**y fyue wittis y haue mys spende
  þoruƷ pride, enuie, & leccherie :
To þe ten heestis y haue not tende
132   þoruƷ slouþe, wraþþe, & glotenie.
¶ In coueitise lyued haue y,
  And neuere dide werkis of mercyes ;
God ! Ʒeue me grace or þat y die !
136   þi merci may passe riƷtwisnes."

Merci Ʒaf him penaunce stronge,
  And seide "man, wolt þou þis take ?
þou muste suffre boþe riƷt and wrong ;
140   If þou þi synne wolt forsake,
¶ In good praiers þou muste wake,
  And neuere ¹ wilne to do a-mys ;
And for þi sorewe þat þou doost make,
144   Merci schal passe riƷtwisnes."

Þe synner took penaunce wiþ good entent,
  And lefte al his wickid synne ;
Whanne he hadde leeue, away he went

7 *

and all his
friends ;
did great penance,
and no sin wil-
fully.
He trusted to
God to bring him
to heaven.

148   From alle his freendis, kiþ & kynne.

¶ In greet penaunce he putte him inne,

And neuere aftir wilfulli dide mys ;

He truste on god heuen to wynne,

152   þere mercy passiþ riȝtwijsnes.

Lord ! give us
grace, and be
merciful to us.

Almiȝti god ! now make us stable,

And ȝeue us grace weel to spede,

And to us alle bee merciable,

156   And forȝeue us alle oure mysdede.

Mary, guide our
souls to thy Son,

¶ And helpe us, ladi, att oure moost nede,

To þi sone oure soulis þou wys,

where Mercy pre-
vails over Justice.

And with his mercy fulli us fede

160   þere mercy passiþ riȝtwijsnes.   A-M-E-N.

["As resoun rewlid," or "Filius Regis Mortuus est," follows. It is printed in *Political, Religious, and Love Poems*, p. 205, &c.]

The Belief.

[*Lambeth MS. 853, ab.* 1430 A.D., *page* 39 ; *written without breaks.*]

¶ **Memento homo quod cinis es, et in cinerem reuerteris.**

Remember, man, that thou art dust.

¶ **Fac bene dum viuis. Post mortem viuere si uis.**

Do well while thou livest.

¶ **Tangere qui gaudet. meretricem qualiter audet.**

How does he who delights to touch a harlot, dare to handle the King of Salvation with polluted hands.

Palmis pollutis, regem tractare salutis.

Credo in deum patrem omnipotentem.

I<small>N</small> þee, god fadir, I bileeue,

    þe firste persoone ful of myȝt,

þat al of nouȝt hast maad to meeue,

4   boþe heuen & erþe, day & nyȝt.

I believe in God the Father,

¶ And in þin oonly goten sone,

    Born of þi silf bifor al þing,

Oure lord ihesus, þe secunde persoone,

8   Boþe oo god in heuen beinge.

and in His only begotten Son,

Jesu Christ, one with God,

¶ þe same god þat euere haþ ben,

    And siþen conceyued bi þe holi goost,

And born of a mayden cleene,

12   Bicause a man in meeknes moost.

conceived by the Holy Ghost, and born of a pure virgin,

[Page 40.]

¶ And riȝt as in þe trynyte

    Ben persoones þre, substauncis but oon,

Riȝt so in þee ben substauncis þre,

16   God, soule, bodi, & al oon persoone.

(of three substances, God, soul, body)

who suffered
under Pontius
Pilate, was
crucified,

¶ Undir pilate þou suffridist peyne
  Bi fre wil, mankinde to saue,
Nailid on a croos, & þeron slain,

and buried,

20   And taken doun & biried in graue.

descended into
hell,

¶ In soule oonli þou wente to helle,
  & took þens þi part, it was good riȝt,

but rose again
the third day,

But up þou roos in fleisch and in felle
24   þe þrid day bi godli myȝt.

ascended into
heaven,

¶ þou stiȝ to heuen in þi manhede,
  And þere þou sittist on þi fadir riȝt side,
But ouer al-where is þi godhede,
28   þere is noon þat from þee him may hide.

whence He shall
come to judge
both quick and
dead.

¶ þens schalt þou come us alle to deeme,
  Boþe quik and dede of adams seed.
With opene woundis & visage breme ;
32   þis bileeue makiþ true men drede.

[1 Page 41.]
I believe in the]
Holy Ghost,

¶ I bileeue in þe holi ¹goost,
  þe þridde persoone in trynyte,
Of which þre noon is more ne moost,
36   But al oon god in persoones þre.

who makes Holy
Church, by faith-
ful men giving
each to other
what each can.

¶ þe holi goost makiþ holi chirche
  Of feiþful men, bi comynynge
Ech oon to oþir what þei kunne worche
40   In holines and good lyuyng.

I believe in the
Forgiveness of
Sins (through the
Sacrament),

¶ Forȝeeuenes y bileeue of synne
  Bi þe holi goost and þe sacrament,
If y maye goostli to hem wynne,
44   Or ellis him silfe is euere present.

¶ þouȝ he neuere so present be,
  ȝit he wole for ful meekenes

þat y do þerto þat is in me,

48   Lest contempt lette me of forȝeuenes.

¶ Also y bileeue in hool mynde,
    þe holi goost schalle knytte aȝen
    þe soule to þe fleische of al mankinde ;

52   For al fleish schal ryse þat deeþ hath slayn.

and that the Holy Ghost shall knit again all men's souls to their flesh on their resurrection,

¶ þe holi goost schal ȝeue also
    Euerlastynge lijf to alle true men.
þat we may heere serue þer-to,

56   ¶ Y rede we seie alle, amen.

and shall give everlasting life to all true men.

[*The Sixteen Points of Charity*, or "Man, among þi myrþis," printed p. 114, below, follows here in the MS.]

The Ten Commandments.

[Lambeth MS. 1853, ab. 430 A.D., page 47 ; written without breaks.]

Every one should teach his children these, and keep them himself.

EUery man schulde teche þis lore
    To hise children with good entent,
And do it him-silf euermore,
4   To kepe weel goddis comaundement.

I. Have no false gods. Worship God Almighty.

¶ Fals goddis þou schalt noon haue,
    But worschipe god omnipotent ;
Make not þi god þat man haþ graue :
8   þis is þe firste comaundement.

II. Take not God's name in vain. Swear by no created thing.

¶ Goddis name in ydil take þou not,
    For if þou do þou schalt be scheent ;
Swere bi no þing þat god haþ wrouȝt :
12   þis is þe secunde comaundement.

III. Hallow the Holy Day.

¶ Haue mynde to helewe þin holi day,
    þou & alle þine with good entent ;
Leue seruile werkis & nyce aray :
16   þis is þe þridde comaundement.

IV. Honour thy Father and Mother.

[¹ Page 41.]

¶ Worschipe þi fadir & þi modir boþe,—
    þat longe lijf to þee be lent,—
With meete ¹and drink, coumfort & cloþe :
20   þis is þe iiij^e comaundement.

V. Kill no man,

¶ Sle no man with yuel wille,
    Ensaumple, or tunge, or strokis dent ;

But euermore do good for ille :

24 þis is þe fifthe comaundement.

but do good for ill.

¶ Do no leccherie in al þi lijf ;
Lete fleischeli knowynge from þee be lent
Saue oonli bi-twene man & wijf :

28 þis is þe sixte comaundement.

VI. Commit not adultery or fornication.

¶ þou schalt not stele no maner of þing,
Ne helpe þerto bi no consent.
Leue alle fals mesuris & al gilinge :

32 þis is þe .vij. comaundement.

VII. Steal not.

Use no deceit.

¶ þou schalt beere no fals witnes
For no mater þat may be ment ;
Seie euere þe soþe, or holde þi pees :

36 þis is þe .viij. comaundement.

VIII. Bear no false witness.

¶ þou schalt not coueite þi neiʒboris good,
As hous, lond, catel, ne rent,
In hindringe of him & of his blood :

40 þis is þe .ix. comaundement.

IX. Covet not thy neighbour's goods.

¶ þou schalt not desire þi neiʒboris feere,
Ne falsli his seruaunt from him hent,
Ne no good þat ¹he hath heere :

44 þis is þe .x. comaundement.

X. Covet not thy neighbour's wife; take not his servant or goods falsely.
[¹ Page 49.]

¶ þese ten to kepe, þou ʒeue us grace
þat on þe roode was al to-rent,
In-to his blis þat we mowe passe

48 At þe laste day of Iugement.

Christ, give us grace to keep these Ten

that we may pass to bliss.

["I Warne eche lijf," p. 107, &c., of this print, follows here in the MS.]

Kepe Wel Cristes Comaundement.

[*Vernon MS., ab.* 1370 A.D., *fol.* 408 *b., col.* 1. *Printed here for comparison' sake, with the metrical points, but no stops.*]

I warne vche leod. þat liueþ in londe.
And do hem dredles. out of were.
þat þei most studie. and vnderstonde.
4 þe lawe of crist. to loue and lere.
þer nis no mon. fer ne nere.
þat may him seluen. saue vn-schent.
But he þat casteþ. wiþ concience clere.
8 To kepe. wel. Cristes Comaundement.

þow most haue o God. and no mo.
And serue him boþe. with mayn and miht.
And ouer alle þinges. loue him also.
12 For he haþ lant þe. lyf and liht.
ʒif þou beo nuyʒed. day or niht.
In peyne be meke. and pacient.
And rule þe ay. be reson riht.
16 And kep wel. Cristes Comaundement.

¶ And let þi neiʒhebor. frend and fo.
Riht frely. of þi frendschupe fele.
In herte. þat þou wilne hem so.
20 Riht as þou woldest. þi self weore wele.
And help to sauen hem. from vneele.
So þat heore soules. beo not schent.
And also heore care. þou helpe to kele.
24 And kepe wel. Cristes comaundement.

Kepe Weel Cristis Comaundement.

[*Lambeth MS.* 853, *ab.* 1430 A.D., *page* 49 ; *written without breaks.*]

I Warne eche lijf þat liueþ in lond
    And do him dredlees out of were,
þat he must studie & vndirstonde
4   þe lawe of god to loue & lere.
  ¶ For þere is no man feer ne neer
    þat may him sillfe saue vnschent
    But he þat castiþ him *with* conscience clere
8   To kepe weel cristis comaundement.

Thou schalt haue oon god & no mo,
    And serue him boþe wiþ mayn & myȝt,
And ouer al þing loue him also,
12   For he haþ lent þee lijf & liȝt.
  ¶ If þou be noied bi day or nyȝt,
    In peyne be meeke & pacient,
    And rewle þee ay bi resoun riȝt,
16   And kepe weel cristis comaundement.

Lete þi neiȝe-'boris, boþe freend & fo,
    Freli of þi freendschip feele ;
In herte wilno þou hem also
20   Riȝt as þou woldist þi silf were wele.
  ¶ Helpe to saue hem from vnsele
    So þat her soulis ben not schent,
    And her care þou helpe to kele,
24   And kepe weel cristis comaundement.

Marginal notes:

Every man must take care to love the Law of God.

Only he can be saved who gives himself to keep Christ's Commandments.

I. Thou shalt have one God,

and love Him above everything.

Be patient in suffering.

[¹ Page 50.] Love thy neighbour as thyself;

and help to save him from all ill.

¶ In Idel. Godes nome tak þou nouȝt.
But cese. and saue þe from þat synne.
Swere bi no þing. þat God haþ wrouht.
28   Be war. his wraþþe. lest þou hit wynne.
But bisy þe her. bale to blynne.
þat blaberyng are wiþ opes blent.
Vncouþe *and* knowen. *and* of þi kynne.
32   And kep wel. cristes comaundement.

¶ In clannes and in cristes werk.
Haue mynde. to holden þin haly day.
And drauh þe þenne. from dedes derk.
36   Wiþ al þi meyne. Mon and may.
And men vnsauȝte. loke þou assay.
To sauȝten hem þenne. at on assent.
And pore and seke. þou plese *and* pay.
40   And kepe wel cristes Comaundement.

¶ þi Fader þi Moder. þou worschupe boþe.
ȝif þou wolt boteles. bale eschcuwe.
With counseil cum-forte hem. with mete *and*
         cloþe.
44   As þou sest. hem neodeþ newe.
And ȝif þei talke of tales vn-trewe.
þou torn hem out. of þat entent.
And cristes lawe. help þat þei knewe.
48   And kep wel cristes. Comaundement.

¶ Sle no mon. wiþ wikked wille.
Be war. and vengeaunce tak þou non.
In word. ne dede. loude. ne stille.
52   Bakbyte þou no mon. blod ny bon.
But ay let gabbynges. glyde and gon.
A-wey wher þei wol. glace. or glent.
And help þat alle men ben aton.
56   And kep wel cristes comaundement.

Goddis name in ydil take þou nouȝt,
    But ceesse & saue þee from þat synne;
Swere bi no þing þat god haþ wrouȝt,
28   Be waar his wrappe lest þou so wynne.
    ¶ But bisie þee euere her bale to blinne
        þat wiþ blaberinge oopis ben blent,
    Vncouþe & knowen of þi kynne;
32   And kepe weel cristis comaundement.

> II. Take not God's name in vain.
>
> Swear by no thing that God has made,
>
> but keep from the bale of blabbering oath-swearers.

In clennes and in cristis werk
    Haue mynde to halowe þin holi daye,
And drawe þee þanne from dedis derk
36   Wiþ al þi meyne, man & may.
    ¶ Men vnsoft, loke þou asay
        To soften ¹them to good assent,
    Helpe poore and sike to please & pay,
40   And kepe weel cristis comaundement.

> III. Hallow thy Holy Day, with
>
> all thy household.
>
> Try to soften unsoft men,
>   [1 Page 51.]
> and to help the poor and sick.

Þi fadir & modir worschipe boþe—
    If þou wolt botelees bale eschewe—
With councelle, coumforte, meete & cloþe,
44   As þou seest þat hem nediþ newe.
    ¶ And if þei talke of wordis vntrewe,
        þou turne hem out of þat entent,
    And cristis lawe helpe þat þei knew,
48   And kepe weel cristis comaundement.

> IV. Honour thy Father and Mother with
>
> counsel, food, and clothes.
>
> Turn them from untrue words, and help them to know Christ's law.

Sle no man with wickid wille;
    Be waar, of veniaunce take þou noon;
Eerli ne late, lowde ne stille,
52   Bacbite no man, blood ne boon,
    ¶ But lete euere gabbing glide & goon
        Away, wheþer it wole glase or glent;
    And helpe þat alle men were at oone,
56   And kepe weel cristis comaundement.

> V. Slay no man: take no vengeance.
>
> Backbite no one,
>
> but let gabbing go by.
>
> Help on peace.

¶ Stele þou nouȝt. þi neiȝebors þing.
Nouþur wiþ stillenes. ne wiþ strif.
Nor with no maner. wrong getyng.
60   þi self þi seruaunt. child. ne wyf.
To sulle and buye. ȝif þou be ryf.
Wayte al way. þat wrong be went.
As þou wolt lyue. þe lastyng lyf.
64   þou kepe wel. cristes comaundement.

[Col. 2.]

Fals witnesse. loke þow non bere.
ȝif þow wolt. in blisse a-byde.
þi neiȝebore. wityngly to dere.
68   Ne no mon nouþer. in no syde.
But loke þat no mon. be a nuyȝed.
And þou may him. from harmes hent.
And help þat falshede. beo distruiet.
72   And kep wel. cristes comaundement.

¶ Sunge þou not. in lecherie.
Such lust vn leueful. let hit pas.
Consente þou not. to such folye.
76   þat founden is so foul trespas.
And loke. þat nouþer more ne las.
þi lykyng. on þat lust be lent.
Leste þou synge. þis songe allas.
80   For brekyng. of cristes comaundement.

¶ þi neiȝhebors wyf. coueyte þou nouȝt.
Vnleuefully. a-ȝeynes þe lawe.
Wiþ hire to sunge. in word ne þouȝt.
84   And from þat deede. euer þou þe drawe.
And neuer sey. to hire no sawe.
To make hire. to synne assent.
Ne plese hire not. with no mis plawe.
88   But kep wel. cristes comaundement.

Synne þou not in leccherie ;
    Such lust vnleefful, lete it passe ;
Consente þou not to þat folie
60   þat founden it is so ¹foule a trespase.
    ¶ And loke þou, neiþer more ne lasse
        þi likinge on þat lust be lent,
    Lest þou singe þis song ' alas
64   For brekinge of cristis comaundement.'

VI. Sin not in Lechery and unlawful lust;

[¹ Page 52.]

set not thy liking on it

lest thou repent it.

Stele þou nouȝt of þi neiȝboris þing
    Neiþer wiþ stilnes ne with strijf,
Ne with no maner of wrong geetynge,
68   þi silf, þi seruaunt, child, ne wijf.
    ¶ To bie & sille if þou be rijfe,
        Loke euere þat wrong away be went :
    If þou wolt han euerlastinge lijf,
72   Kepe weel cristis comaundement.

VII. Steal nothing of thy neighbour's.

Cheat not in buying and selling.

Fals witnes, loke þat þou noon bare ;
    If þou wolt in blis a-bide,
þi neiȝbore wilfulli þou ne dere,
76   Ne noon þat woneþ þee biside ;
    ¶ But loke þat no man be anoied
        If þou may him from harmes hent,
    And helpe þat falshede were distroied,
80   *And* kepe weel cristis comaundement.

VIII. Bear no false witness. Injure not thy neighbour, but keep every one from harm. Help to destroy falsehood.

Þi neiȝboris wijf coueite þou nouȝt
    Vnleeffulli aȝens þe lawe
Wiþ hir to synne in dede or þouȝt,
84   But from þe dede euere þou drawe,
    ¶ And ceesse, & seie to hir no sawe
        To make hir for to synne assent,
    Ne please hir not with no nyce plawe,
88   But kepe weel cristis comaundement.

IX. Covet not thy neighbour's wife, [Page 53.]

and say and do nothing to make her assent to sin.

¶ þi neiȝhebors hous. wenche ne knaue.
Vnskilfully. coueyte þou nouht.
Ne ȝit his good. with wrong to haue.
92   For hit. lest þou to bale be brouht.
For whon þe soþe. schal vp be souht.
ȝif þou in to þis sunnes assent.
Ful bitterly. hit mot be bouȝt.
96   For brekyng of cristes. Comaundement.

¶ Vche mon þat wol. þis lessun lere.
And loueþ. a laweful lyf. to lede.
He may not misse. on none manere.
100   þe merþe of heuene. to his mede.
For crist him here. wol helpe and hede.
And heþene. in to heuene hent.
For þi I. preye. þat crist vs spede.
104   Kuyndely to kepe. his comaundement.

Thi neiʒboris hous, wenche, ne knawe,
 Vnleeſſulli coueite þou nouʒt,
Ne oþir good, wrong to haue,
92 Lest þou for it to bale be brouʒt.
 ¶ For whanne þe sooþe schal be up souʒt,
  If þou to þis synne assent,
 Ful bittirli it schal be bouʒt
96 For brekinge of cristis comaundement.

Covet not thy
neighbour's
house, maid, or
man,

for at the Last
Day thou shalt
pay bitterly for it.

Ech man þat wole þis lessoun lere,
 And loueþ a lawful lijf to lede,
He ne may mys on no manere
100 þe myrþis of heuen to haue to meede ;
 ¶ For crist wole him heere helpe at nede,
  For from hens to heuene he wole him hent,
 For-þi praie we þat crist us spede
104 Kindeli to kepe his comaundement. Amen.

No man who
learns this lesson
can miss the joys
of heaven,

for Christ will
take him there.
Let us pray Him
that we may keep
His Command-
ments.

["There is no creatour but oon," printed pp. 18-21, follows
here in the MS.]

The Sixtene Poyntis of Charite.

[Lambeth MS. 853, ab. 1430 A.D., page 42; written without breaks, except lines 6-12, 21-4.]

Man, remember
whence thou
camest, and
whither thou
goest,

MAn, among þi myrþis haue in mynde
    From whens þou come & whidir þou teendis,
How freelli þou fallist & filist þi kinde !
4   Arise & make of þi mys ameendis,

and that hereafter
thou may'st see
thy Lord as His
chosen child in
Charity.

¶ þat of þis world whanne þou out wendis,
    þou maist in heuene þi lord god se
Among hise apostolis & dere freendis
8   As a chosen child in charitee.

Man's highest
task is to live a
just life.

The hiȝest lessoun þat man may lere
    Is to lyue iust lijf, if þou wolt loke,
Yf þou haue grace to holde & heere,
12   Is playnli printid in poulis booke.

God told St Paul

in the third
heaven the 16
points of Charity.

¶ For god to poul þis lessoun tooke
    in þe þridde heuen, hiȝest of þre,
Euery man to cunne & looke
16   þe sixtene propirtees of charitee.

Though I speak
with angels'
tongues, and have
not Charity, I am
but as a brazen
cymbal.

'**T**houȝ y speke,' seiþ seint poule,
    'As aungils doon, or with mennis tunge,
If charite be not in þi soule,
20   I am but as a brasen symbal song.

[Page 43.]
And though I can
move mountains,
I am worthless if
I want Charity.

¶ And þouȝ my bileeue be neuere so strong
    So þat mounteyns be meued bi seiþ of me,
I am not worthi to god so longe
24   As me wantiþ charite.

Thouȝ y to poore men ȝeue al my good,
   And my bodi to brenne þere hoot fier ys,
And charite be not in my mood,
28   It profitiþ me not to heuen blis.'
   ¶ But for god wolde it schulde not mys
      To knowe in charite whanne we be,
      He tauȝte poul to teche al his
32   þe .xvj. Poyntis of charite.

And though I give my body to be burned, and have not Charity, it profits nothing.

God told Paul to teach his disciples the 16 points of Charity.

'Charite,' he seiþ, 'is pacient,
   Alle disesis meekli suffringe,
Benigne also in hir entent,
36   Kindelid with fier of good lyuyng;
   ¶ Neuere enuyose for ony þing
      To freend ne foo, wheþir it be,
      But euere glad to goddis plesing
40   To cherische alle men in charitee.

1. Charity is patient, and

2. Benign,

3. Never envious,

Charite dooþ neuere wickidli
   Bi purpos of wil, ne wickid dede,
Ne blowen ¹is with pride þouȝ sche be welþi,
44   For to greue god is hir moost drede ;
   ¶ For in helle depe schal be her meede,
      A low wiþ lucifir for to be
      þat for blynde pride wole take noon hede
48   lowli to lyue in charite.

4. Never does wickedly,
5. Is not puffed
¹ [Page 44.]
up with pride,

Charite is not coueitose toold
   Of worschipe ne of wronge wynnynge,
For wiþ ypocritis sche may not holde,
52   Ne consente with wrong getyng.
   ¶ Sche sechiþ not hir owne þing
      for hindringe of neiȝboris þat myȝte be,
      For manye perels ben in pletynge
56   þat acorden not with charitee.

6. Desires no honour or wrong gains,

7. Seeketh not her own,

8 *

Charitee wole no þing be wrooþ
    For harmes þat hir silf may hent,
But for to synne, al oonli is hir looþ,
60   Aȝens goddis comaundement.

¶ Charitee þenkiþ noon yuel in hir entent,
    But stintiþ strijf, & stoondiþ free ;
Al yuel wil, it wolde were went,
64   And chaungid al for charite.

Of wickidnes charite is not glad,
    Bi lauȝter ne bi no likinge,
But euere sobre, soft, & sad,
68   In þouȝt, in word, & in worching.

¶ To riȝt & troupe is hir ioiyng,
    To maynteine truþe where-euere sche be,
Wiþ feiþful and true folk Is hir dwelling,
72   For suche ben chosen in charite.

Alle þingis sche beriþ vp meekeli,
    For al hir wronge schal turne to game ;
Sche falliþ not vnder for vilonye,
76   For los, for sijknes, ne for schame.

¶ Alle þingis sche trowiþ wiþ-out fame
    þat goddis lawe techiþ truþe to be,
And bidiþ þerbi for ony blame,
80   For suche ben children of charitee.

Alle þingis sche hopiþ to haue in blis ;
    For suche sche suffriþ & scrueþ heere ;
For of mercy sche may not mys
84   þat þis lesson wole loue & lere.

¶ Sche abidiþ alle þingis with good chere
    þouȝ sche þinke longe þe eende to se,

For of reward sche haþ ¹no were
88   þat þus abidiþ in charite.

Charite falliþ neuere a-way
 From him þat it in charite wole holde,
Bifore ne aftir domys day,
92   But encresiþ in blis an hundrid folde.
 ¶ Whanne al tresour is tried & tolde,
     Al help to blis is in þese þre,
 Feiþ, hope, & charite, noþing colde ;
96   þe mooste of hem is charite.'

16. Charity never faileth.

All help to bliss is in these three: Faith, hope, charity : and the greatest of these is charity.

Bi charite, man, þou must loue more
 God þan silf, þe sooþ to say,
For þis is þe lord-is owne lore,
100   With al þi power him please & pay ;
 ¶ Thi neiȝbore also, wiþ-oute nay,
     Loue as þi silf saaf to bee ;
 To freend & fo holde faste þi fay,
104   And chaunge þou neuere fro charite.

It makes thee love God above thyself,

and thy neighbour as thyself.

If we þis lessoun we loue & leere,
 And take it truli to oure entent,
We schulen haue knowinge good & cleere
108   Who ben blamelees & who ben schent.
 God, þat hast us oure lijf lent,
     Graunte þat we may oure ¹ silf to enserche
     & se,
 As þou for us on roode were rent,
112   þou chese us to þee for charite. A-M-E-N.

If we learn this lesson, we shall know who will be blessed and who punished.

God grant that [¹ Page 47.]

Christ may choose us, for His love.

["Euery man schulde teche þis lore," printed p. 104-5, follows
here in the MS.]

Quindecim Signa ante diem Judicij.

[*MS. B.* 11. 24, *Trinity College, Cambridge ;*
ab. 1450, A.D.]

<table>
<tr><td>Lord of Heaven,</td><td></td><td>Kynge of grace, & ful of pyte,</td></tr>
<tr><td>have mercy on us!</td><td></td><td>Lord of heuyn, I-blyssyd þou be !</td></tr>
<tr><td></td><td></td><td>Haue mercy on vs, we the beseche,</td></tr>
<tr><td></td><td>4</td><td>Or we lese our wytt & speche !</td></tr>
<tr><td>I will tell of the xv. Signs before Doomsday.</td><td></td><td>xv. tokenys telle I may</td></tr>
<tr><td></td><td></td><td>That shal come before doomys day,</td></tr>
<tr><td></td><td></td><td>As it is seyde yn the prophecye,</td></tr>
<tr><td></td><td>8</td><td>In the book of Jeremye.</td></tr>
<tr><td></td><td></td><td>Herkenyth now þe tokenynge</td></tr>
<tr><td>I. Rain shall fall, bitter as gall,</td><td></td><td>That þe firste day shal brynge :</td></tr>
<tr><td></td><td></td><td>Fro heuyn shal a rayne falle,</td></tr>
<tr><td></td><td>12</td><td>Hit shal be byttyr as eny galle,</td></tr>
<tr><td>red as blood,</td><td></td><td>Hytt shall be as red as any blod,</td></tr>
<tr><td></td><td></td><td>Ouyr all þe worlle a grymly flod ;</td></tr>
<tr><td>and overwhelm the whole world,</td><td></td><td>Hytt schàlle ouergo wyth large mett</td></tr>
<tr><td></td><td>16</td><td>Alle that ys in erth I-sett :</td></tr>
<tr><td>and terrify children unborn.</td><td></td><td>The chylderyn vn-born Aferd shall be</td></tr>
<tr><td></td><td></td><td>Of thys tokenynge, as I telle the,</td></tr>
<tr><td></td><td></td><td>And meue hem tyll our Syth</td></tr>
<tr><td></td><td>20</td><td>Ryth as þey speke myth.</td></tr>
<tr><td>II. The Stars shall fall from heaven.</td><td></td><td>The secunde day ys stronge with alle :</td></tr>
<tr><td></td><td></td><td>The sterrys shal fro heuyn falle,</td></tr>
<tr><td></td><td></td><td>So dredfulle and so breyth</td></tr>
<tr><td></td><td>24</td><td>As the fyre off þe dondyr lyth.</td></tr>
</table>

Men schalle say, " welle-away !
Thys ben the tokenys off domys day ! "
They schall cry & syke sore,

28　And say, " lord, mercy, thyn ore¹! "

[¹ MS. thynore]

III. The Sun

The iij^{de} day ys off syche :
In erthe and in heuyn-ryche
The hye son thatt ys so bryth,

32　So fayr, and so full off lyth,

shall turn black
as pitch.

Hitt shalle be swarte as any pyche :
Alle thatt shall be rewlyche.
Men schalle þen sone se

36　Att mydday hytt shalle swarte be ;
All thatt ben on lyve
Schalle thys wordys dryve.
" Alas thatt we scholle Abyde

40　To se þis sorowe in Euery syde ! "

IV. Everything

The iiij^{te} day ys swythe longe,
With wepynge & wyth sorow Amonge :

on earth shall
turn into red
blood

All þat in erthe stonde

44　Schall to red blod wende ;
They schalle drawe hem to þe grownde,
Ther schalle they dwelle butt no stownde,
To the see þey schalle for drede,

and flee to the sea.

48　Ryth as moyses the prophytt sayde,
Thatt the mone schalle rowly falle

The Moon shall
fall from heaven.

And wynd outt of hys reche stalle.
The man schalle say to hys wyff

52　" Alas þatt we be nowe Alyve ! "
The v^{te} day comyth swythe ;

V. All beasts
shall hold up their
heads towards
heaven.

For euery best þatt ys on lyve,
Toward heuyn her hedd schall holde.

56　For thatt wonþer As y yowe tollde,
Men schalle say, " lord, thyn ore

Men shall pray
God mercy,

Off our sorowe & off our sore ! "
Thys tellyth the prophecy

60　In þe booke of Jeromy.

Welle we schalle vndyrstonde
Thatt cristyndom hatt vnperfonge.

"Thatt day, Ihesus to vs se

64 As þou¹ vs bowtyst vppon a tre,
Thatt we may com to þy blysse
Lord, when þy wille ys !"

The vj day schall down Falle

68 The treys with þe croppys alle,
And toward þe erthe the croppys schalle be.
For fere the man schalle lese hys wyff,

The wyff her chyld, þe chylld hys lyff ;

72 Alle thatt leve schall lese here wytte ;
Wo they be thatt schalle a-byde hytte,
Bettyr they were to be oute off lyve
Than soche payne for to dryve.

76 The vij day schalle fall down
Chyrche and castelle and euery town² ;

All schall to-breke ; and euery hylle
Shalle lowe, valeys For to Fylle ;

80 The erthe schalle [be] shene and clene ;
In þis worlle alle schalle be evyn ;
Than schalle þe worlle evyn be :
Wo ys he þat thatt schalle se !

84 The viij day ys a day off drede,
Ryth as moyses þe prophytt seyde

Thatt the see woll ryse & fle,
Thatt euery best aferd schall be ;

88 Than for drede hytt woll ryse & flowe
With wawys grete, & stormys towe :

Thorowe the strength off þe wynd
Into the Welken hitt schall slynge ;

92 All thatt leuyth þatt day

Wold fle away, but þey ne may ;

Vndyr erthe I-hydd they wold be
Thatt Ihesu cryst scholl nott hem Ase.

96 Then wolle the see wytdrawe,

And wend to hys owyn hawe.

Godd of heuyn, þat best may,

Haue mercy on vs vppon þatt day !

100   The ix day, wondyr hytt ys,

As the prophecy tellyth hytt I wys :

Thatt all þynge schall speke þan,

And cry in erthe aftyr þe steuyn off man,

104   And be-mone hem self in owr syȝth

Ryth as þey speke myth.

Lord Ihesu, thy myth þou fullfelle !

We be sorry þatt we dede agayn þi wille

108   Or with towyth or with dede.

Lord Ihesu ! brenge vs oute of þis drede

Thatt we may com to rest !

Ther bale ys most, & bote ys nexte.

112   The .x. day ys day of welaway

As gregory sayth, and Jeromy :

Than schalle knele þe angelys bryth

Before þe face of godd allmyth.

116   Seynt peter, noþer his felow-redde,

Dar nott speke A word for drede ;

They schalle se heuyn vngo,

And þe erthe schall Also,

120   They schalle schryke & crye lome

For þe drede of þe grett dome.

Develyn schall com oute off helle

As seynt Johan doyth vs tell,

124   They schalle kry, " lord, thyn ore

Off our sorowe & of our sore !

Lett vs to heuyn com !

Longe þou hast hytt vs be-nome

128   For our gylt, and our mysdede,

And for our awyn wykkyd rede ! "

Thys ys a day of moche sorowe ;

A strongyr comyth on the morrowe.

132   The xi day comyth lyche,

With stronge stormys sykyrlyche,

And alle the stonys moche & lyte

Scholle to-gedyr sore smyte ;

136 Alle the worlle schalle to-dryve ;

Wo be þey þatt ben on lyve !

The rayn bowe Iwryyd schalle be,

Grymlyche In syȝth for to see.

140 Than the deuelyn schalle swyde ren,

And for fere to helle torn ;

God wille say, " ther schull ye be,

Ther schall ye wone & be war,"

144 God grownte so to be-tyde

Thatt we may be on bettyr syde !

The xij day ys dredfulle than,

For than was neuer schappe of man

148 That wolle þatt god dyd hym ryth

Yff he dyrst, & most of myth.

Angelys thatt hym seruyn alle

Scholl for vs vppon kneys falle

152 To goddys feett for our syn ;

And for the loue of all man kyn.

Lord we be-seche the

In þi mercy for to be !

156 Dredfully comyth the xiij day

To all þatt Abyde hytt may.

Fro the begynnynge of Adamys com

Tylle the end of þe day of doome,

160 Ne myth no man in booke rede

Half the sorow, noþer half þe drede,

That god schalle say than

When he comyth down yn schappe of man,

164 For alle the stonys grett and smale

Thatt byth in erthe withoutyn tale,

All they schalle to-gedyr drynge,

And cuerychon to oþer dynge ;

168 They schall ryse & grynd so

Thatt þe fyr fro hem schalle go ;

They schall bren also bryth

As þe fyr of þe dondyr lyth.

172 The xiiij day ys A day of sorowe ;

Stronge fyr schalle com on þe morow,

Ther schalle nothyng in þys worlle leve

Butt schalle bren to morow tyll eve.

176 Thys passyth nott swythe sone ;

On the morow ys þe day of doome.

The xv day comyth swythe :

For euery man þat was on lyve

180 Fro Adamys tyme, the fyrst man,

Alle to þe dome schalle com than,

Euery man of xxxᵗⁱ wynter olde,

All schall com þe dome to be-holde ;

184 Euery man schalle oþere mete

Att the mownte of olevett.

Two angelys schall blowe her bemys ;

The folke schall com alle attonys.

188 Fulle sore than they may Agryse

Whan they shulle to þe dome aryse,

Two angelys schall com be-forne

With þe scorges, and with the crowne of thorn

192 With drewry cher and sory mode

As hytt on hys hedd stode ;

And the sper al so scharpe

As hytt stod on hys hertt.

196 For no enuy, ne for no pryde,

Longeus hym stonge dorow þe syde :

Longeus then styll stode,

On hys fyngorys ran þe blod,

200 He strokyd ther-with hys eyn ryth,

They be-coom as cler as candyllyȝth.

" Kynge and lord full of pyte,

Thys mys-gylt þou for-yeue me !

204 I dyd hyt for non evyll dede,

Noþer for no covetyse of mede."

Angels shall
bring the Cross
and bloody nails.

Angelys schall brenge þe rode bryth,
With blody naylys precyous of syth.

Then Christ, sad,
shall come,

208   Then comyth our lord with drewry mode,
Wyth armys I-spred all on blod :

and say, " Man,
see what I
suffered for thee !
I was

" Man, now þe soth þou mayst I-se,
Whatt I sufferd her for the.

212   Thys passyon I sufferd her for þe :

crowned with
thorns.
And thou lovedst
to swear by My
eyes, hair, and
pains,

I-cronyd I was with thornys of a tre ;
Thys was to the leff for to swere
Be my eyn & be myn here,

216   And be my paynys that wher stronge.
Man, hytt was þe fulle ryve

My five wounds,

To swere be my wowndys fyve,

teeth, tongue,

Be my tethe And my tonge,

heart, lungs,

220   Be my hertt and be my longe,
Hytt thowyth the fulle grett pryde

side, brains and
head,
      [1 ? heved]
nay, My soul.

For to swere be my syde,
Be my brayne & be my hedd ; [1]

224   be my sowle I was ofte be-revyd.

Such shame thou
didst me !

Man, hytt was full grett dyspyte
So offte to make me edwyte !

Thou wouldst not
feed or help me.

Thou woldyst nott clothe me, ne fede,

228   Thou woldyst nott helpe me att my nede !

What hast thou
suffered for Me ? "

Man offte þou hast for-sworn me !
Man what sufferst þou for me ? "

Then comes Our
Lady, weeping

Than comyth our lady hem be-fore—

232   In blyssyd tyme was she I-bore—

tears of blood,

With terys rennynge alle on blodd,
Sore wepynge with drewry modd ;

and saying,

" Fadyr, & son, and holygost,

" King and Lord,
my sweet Son,
      [2 thee]

236   Kynge and lord as þou wost,
My swete son, I praye de [2]

grant me to-day
my prayer.
Lose not Thy
handiwork

My bone to day þou grawnt me !
Thy honde warke þat þou hast wrowyth,

240   My dere son, for-lese hem nowhte !

Thou bowst hem wyth þy blodd

And with þy flessch vppon þe rode ;

My swete son, I pray the

244 For all mankynd þat I may be ;

Graw[n]te hem þy swete blysse,

None of hem þatt þou ne mysse."

"Modyr, thy wille I-fullfyllyd shall be,

248 Thy bone to day I grawnt hytt þe ;

The goode y wille lese nowth,

My hondwerke that I haue wrowth.

Thys þatt wallde nott serue me,

252 My blysse schalle they neuere se,

Into payne they schalle wende,

To haue ³ hytt euere withoutyn ende.

My chyldryn þat haue seruyd me,

256 In my blysse they schall euere be ;

Ye scholl com with me to heuyn

With angelys songe and mery steuyn.

And he clepyth hym be-fore,—

260 In blyssyd tyme wer they I-bore,—

He spekyth to hem myldelyche,

" Comyth with me to my kyngdome ryche."

Lord we be-seche þe

264 Thy swete blysse þatt we mott se ;

When we com to oure lyvys ende,

Into thy blysse þat we mot wende,

And grawnt vs thatt hytt so be !

268 Amen, Amen, lord, For charite !

Side glosses:
bought with Thy blood.

I pray Thee, grant all men Thy bliss ;

miss none ! "

" Mother, thy will shall be done.

I will not lose the good.

Those who would not serve Me

shall go to everlasting torment. [³ *haue* repeated in MS.] My children, who have served Me,

shall come with Me to heaven."

Lord, grant us to see Thy bliss when we die !

Amen !

[For the meaning of l. 182, see Hampole's *Pricke of Conscience,* ed. Morris, 1863, p. 135, lls. 4983-90.
     Þan sal alle ryse in þe same eld þan
     Þat God had fully here als man . . . .
     Þan was he of threty yhere elde, and twa,
     And of thre monethes þar-with alswa ;
     In þat elde alle sal ryse at the last
     When þai here þe grete bemes blast.]

Who can not Wepe, com lerne of me.

(THE VIRGIN'S SONG OVER HER DEAD SON.)

[*MS. O. 9. 38, Trin. Coll. Cambridge.   Written mostly as prose.*]

Sodenly A-frayd, halfe wakynge halfe slepyng,

A woman fair sat weeping
and gretly dysmayd, A woman sate wepyng,

With fauour in here face far passynge my reson,

4   And of here sore wepyng þis was þe encheson ;

over her dead son lying in her lap,
Here sone yn here lappe layd, sche seyd, sleyn
by treson :

yf wepyng myȝt rype be, hit semyd then yn seson.

lamenting how Jesus was robbed of his life,
Ihesus, so sche sobbed,

8   so here sone was bobbed

And of hys lyue robbed ;

saying, 'Who cannot weep, come learn of me.'
Seynge thys wordys as y sey the,

" Who can not wepe, com lerne of me."

"I cannot weep."
12   y seyd y cowde not wepe, y was so hard hertyd.

Sche answerd me schortly with wordys þat
smartyd,

'Nature shall make thee,
" Lo, nature schall meve þe ; thow must be
conuertyd,

thy father is dead ;
thyn owne fadyr thys nyȝth ys dede :" thys
sche twhertyd :

my son is robbed of his life.'
16   " Ihesus, so my sone ys bobbed,

and of hys lyue robbed.

ffor soth then y sobbed

Veryfyyng thys wordys, seyng to the,

20   Who can not wepe com lerne at me."

"Now, broke hert, y the praye ! thys cord lyeth 'Break, my heart!
    so rulye,   for my son so
So betyn, so woundyd, Entretyd so fuly.   foully used.

What wyȝt may be-hold, and wepe not? none Who could see
    truly,   him and not
                                           weep ?'

24   to see my ded dyre sone bledynge, lo, thys
      newly ! "

Euer stylle schee sobbed,   So still she sobbed
So here sone was bobbed   how her son was
And of hys lyue robbed.   slain.

28   Newyng these wordys, as y sey the,
    " Who can not wepe, com lerne at me."

On me sche cast here yee, and seyd, " see, man,
      thy brother ! "

Sche kyste hym, and seyd, "swete, am y not She kissed him;
    thy modyr ? "

32   And swonynge schee fylle ; ther hyt wold be no she swooned ;
    nothyr :

y not whych more dedlye, the tone or the todyr.

yett sche reuyued, and sobbed   and reviving, she
                                          sobbed how her
how here sone was bobbed   son was bobbed,

36   & of hys lyue robbed.

    " Who can not wepe," thys ys the lay,   and then vanished
    And with that wordys schee vanyschyd A-way.∵ away.

                                    ffinis.

𝕿𝖍𝖊 𝕯𝖊𝖆𝖙𝖍 𝖔𝖋 𝕬𝖗𝖈𝖍𝖇𝖎𝖘𝖍𝖔𝖕 𝕾𝖈𝖗𝖔𝖕𝖊

(WHO WAS BEHEADED, 8 JUNE, 1405).

[From MS. R. 4. 20, Trin. Coll. Cambridge, on a blank leaf at the end of Lydgate's Siege of Thebes.]

Wise Bishop
Scrope
is dead,

Hay hay hay hay thynke oñ Whitsonmonday.
The bysshop Scrope that was so wyse
Nowe is he dede and lowe he lyse   hay

but by Mary's
help he may
rise to heaven.

To hevyns blys yhit may he ryse
4   Thurghe helpe of Marie that mylde may

On the hill
he took
his death right
willingly.

Wheñ he was broght vnto the hylle
He held hym̄ both mylde and stylle   hay
He toke his deth *with* fulle gode wylle
8   As I haue herde fulle trewe men say

His executioner
knelt to him
and asked his
forgiveness.

He that shulde his dethe be
He kneled downe vppoñ his kne   hay
Lord *your* deth forgyffe it me
12   Fulle hertly here to yowe I pray

He granted it,
asking for five
strokes
to send him
to heaven.

Here I wylle the com̄mende
yᵘ gyff me fyve strokys *with* thy hende   hay
And theñ my wayes yᵘ latt me wende
16   To hevyns blys that lastys ay

[Compare Hall's Chronicle, *Hen. IV.* fol. xxv (ed. 1550) W. A. W.]

EXTRACT FROM *HALLE* AS TO ARCHBISHOP SCROPE'S
DEATH. ED. 1542 ?(HY. ELLIS) FOL. XXV.

KYNG HENRY THE .IIII.

¶ THE SIXT YERE.

IN this yere the Earle of Northumber- **The vi yere.** **The Earl of Northumberland conspired with**
laude, which bare styll a venemous
scorpion in his cankered heart, and coulde
not desist to inuent and deuise waies and meanes howe
to be reuenged of kyng Henry and his fautours, began
secretely to communicate his interior imaginacions and
priuie thoughtes with Richard Scrop, Archebishop of **Archbishop Scrope.**
Yorke, brother to william lord Scrop, treasorer of
England, whome kyng Henry (as you have heard) be-
headed at the towne of Bristow, and with Thomas **Earl Mowbray.**
Mowberey, erle Marshal, sonne to Thomas duke of
Norffolke, for kyng Henries cause before banished
the realme of England, and with the lordes, Hast-
ynges, Fauconbridge, Bardolfe, and diverse other **and others, against**
whiche he knewe to beare deadly hate and inward
grudge toward the kyng. After long consultacion **Henry.**
had, it was finally concluded and determined amongest **and all agreed to**
theym, that all they, their frendes and alies, with all
their power, should mete at Yorkeswold at a day **meet at Yorkeswold on a day appointed.**
appointed, and that therle of Northumberland should
be chefetaine and supreme gouernour of the armie,
which promised to bring with him a great number of
Scottes.

This sedicious conspiracye was not so secretly kept,
nor so closely cloked, but that the kyng therof had
knowledge, and was fully aduertised. wherfore to pre-
uent the time of their assembly, he, with suche power **But before this Henry marched northwards,**
as he could sodainly gather together, with all diligence

9

marched toward the North parties, and vsed suche a
celeritie in his iourney that he was thither come with
all his hoste and power before the confederates hearde
any inkelyng of his marchyng forward; and sodainly
there wer apprehended the archebishop, the earle
Marshall, sir Iohn Lampley, and sir Robart Plumpton.
These personnes wer arrained, atteinted, and adiudged
to die; and so on the Monday in Whytson weke all
they withoute the Citie of Yorke were beheadded.

Here of necessitie I ought not, nor will not, forgeate
how some foolishe and fantasticall personnes haue
wrytten, howe erronius Ippocrites and sedicyous Asses
haue endited, howe supersticious Fryers and malycious
Monkes haue declared and diuulged—bothe contrary to
goddes doctrine, the honoure of their prince, and
common knowen veritie—that at the howre of the
execucion of this Bishop (which of the Execucioner
desired to haue fiue strokes in remembraunce of the
fiue woundes of Christ) the kyng at the same tyme
syttyng at diner had .v. strokes in his necke by a
person inuisible, & was incontinently striken with a
leprey; which is a manifest lye, as you shall after
plainely perceiue.

What shall a man say of suche writers whiche toke
vpon them to knowe the secretes of Goddes iudgement?
what shall men thinke of suche beastly persones,
whiche, regardyng not their bounden dutie and
obeisance to their prynce & souerain Lorde, enuied the
punishment of traiters and torment of offenders. But
what shall all men coniecture of suche whyche, fauor-
ynge theyr owne worldly dignitie, their owne priuat
auctorite, their owne peculiar profit, wyl thus iuggle,
raile, and imagine fantasies agaynst their soueraigne
lorde and Prince, and put them in memorye as a
miracle to his dyshonor and perpetuall infamy: well
let wyse men iudge what I haue said.

GLOSSARY.

Abic, p. 26, l. 130; p. 96, l. 22, pay for, atone for; A.S. *abicgan*.

Abowe, p. 97, l. 69, bow, bend, humble.

Adwiten, p. 70, l. 396, blame, accuse; A.S. *edwitan*.

Aȝenseid, p. 94, l. 100, denied.

Aggregidist, p. 52, l. 346, *aggreger*, to aggravate. Cotgrave.

Agryse, p. 123, l. 188, A.S. *agrysan*, to fear.

Among, p. 81, l. 59, at intervals, 'amonge, or sum tyme, *interdum, quandoque.*' P. Parv.

Apecle, p. 71, l. 433, Fr. *appeler*, to accuse, appeach, or charge with. Cot.

Aslake, p. 80, l. 47, A.S. *aslacian*, slacken, dissolve.

Aslope, p. 54, l. 427, aside.

Asswage, p. 79, l. 10, quiet down; Fr. *assouvager*, to assuage, quiet, still, pacific. Cot.

Attir, p. 24, l. 62, poisonous.

Auauntage, at his, p. 81, l. 70, in his power, control.

Awaite, p. 76, l. 593, ? watch.

Balke, p. 92, l. 47, baulk, a mess of his life.

Beerde, p. 13, l. 50, woman, maiden.

Beete, p. 12, l. 11, A.S. *gebétan*, to amend, atone for.

Bemys, p. 123, l. 186, trumpets; A.S. *béme*.

Bigoon, p. 16, l. 40, overwhelmed; A.S. *begán*, to go over.

Bihatid, p. 82, l. 24, thoroughly hated.

Bihiȝt, p. 19, l. 52, promised; A.S. *beháten*.

Bikir, p. 46, l. 15, strife.

Binam, p. 92, l. 34, took away from; A.S. *benám*.

Bitake, p. 20, l. 74, commit; A.S. *betæcan*.

Bleere, p. 60, l. 78, mock, scorn; 'I gyue him the best counsayle I can, and the knaue *bleareth* his tonge at me, *tirer la langue.*' Palsgrave.

Blynne, p. 97, l. 66, cease.

Blyue, p. 46, l. 177; p. 96, l. 30, quickly.

Bobbed, p. 126, l. 8, beaten; 'bobet on the heed, *coup de poing.*' Palsgrave.

Boone, p. 6, l. 21, prayer; A.S. *ben*.

9 *

Bote, p. 11, l. 104, remedy ; A.S. *bót*.

Boteles, p. 108, l. 42, remediless.

Breme, p. 102, l. 31, ? not A.S. *breme*, glorious, but ' *brym* or fers. *Ferus, ferox*.' Pr. Parv.

Broode, p. 37, l. 77, abroad, about.

Careful, p. 16, l. 39, full of care and trouble.

Cesoun, p. 42, l. 28, ? scizin, possession, or 'take a cesoun,' stay a season or time.

Chesoun, p. 42, l. 32, cause, reason ; O.Fr. *achaison*, occasion.

Clene, p. 1, l. 7, pure ; ' Clene, *mundus, purus*.' Pr. Parv.

Clennesse, p. 64, l. 197, purity.

Clinge, p. 85, l. 68 ; p. 89, l. 20, A.S. *clingan*, to wither, cling, or shrink up.

Conclude, p. 77, l. 605, shut up.

Contrarie, p. 37, l. 87, go contrary to.

Coorde, p. 38, l. 111, accord, agree.

Coost, p. 34, l. 63, Fr. *costé*, a coast or quarter. Cotgrave.

Countirtaile, p. 71, l. 416, Fr. *contretaille*, the one part of a tallie, or score, alreadie marked, or notched. Cotgrave.

Croppys, p. 120, l. 68, tops ; A.S. *crop*, top, bunch, berry.

Cunne, p. 114, l. 15, A.S. *cunnan*, to know.

Cus, p. 12, l. 22, kiss ; A.S. *cus, cyss*.

Daswen, p. 68, l. 338, become dazed or dim; Du. *duyster*, dim.

Defie, p. 95, l. 6, fear for?

Delice, p. 78, l. 633; Delijs, p. 42, l. 43, Fr. *delices*, delights, pleasures.

Dere, p. 110, l. 67, injure ; A.S. *derian*.

Derworþiest, p. 52, l. 352, A.S. *deorwurde*, precious, of great value.

Diffence, p. 60, l. 63, Fr. *defense*, answer, argument.

Discure, p. 63, l. 165, discover.

Dispence, p. 63, l. 157, gain, reward ?

Disceyuable, p. 86, l. 7, deceitful.

Disperage, p. 74, l. 508, incongruity ; O.Fr. *desparager*, to offer vnto, or impose on, a man vnfit, or vnworthie conditions. Cot.

Dondyr, p. 118, l. 24, thunder.

Drewis, p. 60, l. 66 ? draughts.

Drynge, p. 122, l. 166, A.S. *pringan*, throng, rush.

Dwynne, p. 27, l. 176, dwindle ; A.S. *dwinan*, to pine, fade, waste away.

Edwyte, p. 124, l. 226, reproach, twitting; A.S. *edwite*, reproach, disgrace, contumely.

Encheson, p. 10, l. 75, occasion ; O. French, *achaison*.

Ensure, p. 18, l. 9, cock sure.

Entensioun, p. 21, l. 92, ? excuse, or mind.

Eruest, p. 69, l. 350, harvest; A.S. *hærfest*.

Faite, p. 77, l. 595, ? deceive ; O.Fr. ' *faiteus*, criminel, coupable.'

Fare, p. 95, l. 13, goings on, ways, life.

Fawe, p. 96, l. 28, fain, glad.

Felle, p. 25, l. 92, ? fail, or fell.

Fen, p. 26, l. 121, mire, mud.

Fere, p. 38, l. 111, company ; *in fere*, together.

Fere, p. 86, l. 16, companion, person.

Filist, p. 114, l. 3, defilest.

Flaite, p. 75, l. 532, Du. *vleyden*, to flatter, to sooth, or to entice with faire [words]. Hexham.

Fleme, p. 18, l. 17, banish; A.S. *flyman.*

Florische, p. 89, l. 18, ornament, deck.

Foisoun, p. 43, l. 64, Fr. *foison,* plentie, great fullnesse. Cot.

Fondid, p. 8, l. 23, tried; A.S. *fandian,* to try.

Foondi, p. 95, l. 13, try.

Foonued, p. 96, l. 33, foolish?

For, p. 19, l. 35, 40, because.

Forbeere, p. 60, l. 76, restrain.

Forclonge, p. 18, l. 31, A.S. *clingan,* to wither, pine, or shrink up; *forclungen,* shrunk.

Forlete, p. 30, l. 250, A.S. *forlætan,* to let go.

Forþi, p. 24, l. 89, for that reason.

Foulden, p. 73, l. 485, ?fold, bend.

Frame, p. 44, l. 97, ? A.S. *freme,* profit, advantage.

Frauȝte, p. 76, l. 590, freight, load.

Frike, p. 23, l. 26, glad, joyful; A.S. *frician,* to dance, frisk.

Gesoun, p. 64, l. 206, ? Fr. *gesse,* a common sinke or sewer; a gutter for the voiding of ordure. Cotgr. Not. E. *geason,* rare, strange.

Gist, p. 93, l. 63, show.

Glewe, p. 29, l. 236, A.S *gleow,* joy, mirth, glee.

Grame, p. 63, l. 168, A.S. *grama,* anger, rage, wrath.

Greede, p. 14, l. 73, greet, moan; A.S. *grætan,* to weep, cry out.

Gril, p. 83, l. 12, sharp, unkind; O.N. *grila.* H. Coleridge.

Hadde-y-wist, p. 73, l. 497, had-I-known (what would have happened), after-regret.

Happe, p. 89, l. 26, wrap over, cover for defence; Isl. *hypia,* Jamieson.

Harewide, p. 53, l. 385, tore open.

Hawe, p. 121, l. 97, A.S. *hah,* hole, den.

He, p. 59, l. 39, they.

Hende, p. 7, l. 25, gentle.

Hildande, p. 23, l. 55, beholden.

Hirde, p. 17, l. 52, A.S. *hirde,* a shepherd.

Ho, p. 14, l. 71, halt, stop.

Homeli, p. 63, l. 163, familiar.

Hore, p. 83, l. 13, hoar, hoariness.

Hote, p. 41, l. 15, be called; A.S. *hátan.*

Ilke, p. 23, l. 54, every.

Insiȝt, p. 66, l. 250; p. 69, l. 339, 'insyght, *inspexio, circumspeccio.*' Promptorium.

Kinde, p. 20, l. 59, nature.

Kiþe, p. 11, l. 92, show; A.S. *cydan,* to make known, declare, show.

Kynde, p. 9, l. 53, nature; A.S. *ge-cynd.*

Kyndeli, p. 8, l. 19, natural; A.S. *ge-cyndelic.*

Lappid, p. 3, l. 50, wrapped; 'Lappyn, or whappyn yn clobys (happyn to-gedyr, wrap togeder in clothes). *Involvo.*' P. Parv.

Lauȝt, p. 30, l. 249; p. 76, l. 586, caught, taken; A.S. *læccan,* to seize.

Leeme, p. 52, l. 335, A.S. *leoma,* light, flame.

Leepis, p. 47, l. 181; p. 72, l. 451, A.S. *leap,* a basket, hamper.

Leere, p. 8, l. 5, teach; A.S. *læran.*

Lees, p. 16, l. 45, lies.

Leit, p. 48, l. 226; Leite, p. 52, l. 355, lightning; A.S. *lihting.*

Lende, p. 23, l. 41, lent; A.S. *lened.*

Lent, p. 105, l. 26, put away?; ? A.S. *lengde,* put off, *perf.* of *lengian.*

Lete, p. 28, l. 186, leave, cease ; A.S. *lætan*, let go.

Lewide, p. 67, l. 303, lay, ignorant.

Leye, p. 95, l. 2, field after the crop is cut, *clover ley*, &c. ; ? not A.S. *lagu*, a district in which a certain law was in force.

Likerose, p. 20, l. 55, lecherous.

Likid, p. 8, l. 16, pleased.

Liking, p. 3, l. 50, pleasant.

Likinge, p. 92, l. 49 ; p. 93, l. 77, 81, lust.

Likingly, p. 91, l. 20, pleasantly.

List, p. 4, l. 3 ; A.S. *list*, wisdom, science, power, faculty ; *lyst*, desire, love, admiration.

Lome, p. 121, l. 120, frequently ; A.S. *gelóme*.

Maistrie, p. 20, l. 80, mastery, (see p. 33, l. 58,) ? not tricks.

Mammillis, p. 1, l. 5, breasts, paps ; Pappe, *Mamilla*. P. Parv.

Maugre, p. 65, l. 215, reviling, railing ; Fr. *maugréer*, to curse, reuile extreamly, raile on despightfully.

Mawmetis, p. 45, l. 118, idols.

Medele, p. 20, l. 86, mingle.

Meene, p. 1, l. 4, remember ; A.S. *mænan*.

Meete, p. 1, l. 6, food.

Melle, p. 53, l. 387, meddle.

Mengid, p. 59, l. 51, A.S. *mengian*, mix, mingle.

Mett, p. 118, l. 15, measure ; A.S. *mete*.

Mydmore, p. 83, l. 17, midmorning.

Mynde, p. 9, l. 25, ? mention, or A.S. *myne*, memory.

Mynne, p. 24, l. 78, remember.

Myscheue, p. 90, l. 46, come to grief.

Mystire, p. 76, l. 572, need ; Fr. *mestier*, need, lacke, necessitie, want. Cotgrave.

Nempne, p. 6, l. 7, name ; A.S. *nemnan*.

Newyng, p. 127, l. 28, renewing, repeating.

Nuyȝed, p. 106, l. 13, annoyed, troubled.

Nyce, p. 53, l. 390, Fr. *niais*, a simple, witlesse, and vnexperienced gull. *Nice*, lither, lazie, sloathfull, dull, simple. Cot.

Nym, p. 53, l. 371, take ; A.S. *niman*, to take.

Of, p. 98, l. 101, from.

Ore, p. 119, l. 57, mercy.

Ouerhope, p. 68, l. 331, too much confidence, sanguineness.

Paieth, p. 24, l. 58, pleases.

Pay, p. 14, l. 80, satisfaction, pleasure ; *payé*, satisfied, contented. Cotgrave.

Pilis, p. 64, l. 182, peels, holds, castles.

Piȝt, p. 3, l. 61, pitched ; p. 4, l. 13 ; p. 94, l. 90, placed ; p. 12, l. 16, put, dressed.

Pooste, p. 43, l. 79, power.

Port, p. 93, l. 85, mien.

Prest, p. 45, l. 116, quickly.

Prouȝ, p. 50, l. 288, advantage, profit ; Fr. *prou*.

Pure, p. 18, l. 11, purify.

Pursue, p. 68, l. 328, follow, strive.

Put, p. 73, l. 475, throw, casting.

Queed, p. 6, l. 18, wicked one, devil ; Dutch, *quaad*.

Qwart, p. 23, l. 2, of good heart or cheer ; O.Fr. *quor*, courage.

Qweme, p. 18, l. 15, A.S. *cweman*, to please.

Race, p. 48, l. 238, A.S. *ræs*, rush, attack ; cp. mill*race*.

Raper, p. 88, l. 16, earlier, sooner.

Rapir, p. 86, l. 9, preferable.

Releef, p. 47, l. 181, leavings.

Remewe, p. 20, l. 69, remove.

Rere, p. 70, l. 379, late. *Rere* suppers are complained of in Waddington (b. 1300), Robert of Brunne, 1303, A.D., and many other writers.

Rereage, p. 73, l. 483, arrears.

Reuep, p. 30, l. 257, bereaves, takes away.

Riȝt, p. 46, l. 170, upright, straight.

Rijfe, p. 92, l. 29, much ; Du. *rijf*, rife, abundant.

Romage, p. 93, l. 60, roaming.

Rouȝte, p. 36, l. 38, recked ; A.S. *róhte*.

Rowne, p. 63, l. 163, whisper.

Ruli, p. 10, l. 68, grievous ; p. 89, l. 27, sad, mournful ; A.S. *hreów*, grief, penitence ; *hreów-lic*, cruel, mournful.

Ryve, p. 124, l. 217 (see *rijfe*), customary, frequent.

Sadli, p. 8, l. 7, fixedly.

Sale, p. 57, l. 502 ; Fr. *salle*, hall.

Sauȝte, p. 76, l. 592, A.S. *saht*, reconciled.

Sauȝten, p. 108, l. 38, reconcile ; A.S. *sehtian*. Note the change to *soften* in the later text, p. 109.

Schende, p. 11, l. 118, shame, disgrace, ruin ; A.S. *sceond*, shame, disgrace.

Schendip, p. 53, l. 374, A.S. *scendan*, to confound, shame, reproach, revile.

Schille, p. 65, l. 232 ; schyllo and sharpe, *acutus, sonorus*.

Schowr, p. 44, l. 96, A.S. *scúr*, battle, fight.

Sconfitith, p. 46, l. 154, discomfits.

Scryue, p. 58, l. 2, describe.

Secke, p. 76, l. 589, sack, bag.

See, p. 13, l. 54, seat.

Seelde, p. 41, l. 6, seldom.

Seete, p. 37, l. 89, set.

Sege, p. 2, l. 35, seat ; Fr. *siège*.

Seruile, p. 104, l. 15, of service, of business.

Sijke, p. 78, l. 634, sickness ; Du. *zieck*, sick.

Sikir, p. 33, l. 50, certain, sure.

Skile, p. 9, l. 33, reason ; O.N. *skil*.

Slake, p. 11, l. 112, become slack, cease.

Slidir, p. 49, l. 269, slydyr (or swypyr as a wey). *Lubricus*, P. Parv.

Smerte, p. 93, l. 67, smart, pain, prick.

Soote, p. 29, l. 248, sweet one.

Spaynel, p. 91, l. 4, spaniel ; Fr. *espagneul*, a Spaniell. Cot.

Spousebriche, p. 47, l. 188, adultery.

Spurne, p. 43, l. 76, A.S. *spurnan*, to strike with the heel ; p. 91, l. 11, spurned.

Spute, p. 46, l. 164, dispute.

Stabilte, p. 26, l. 144, fixedness, firmness.

Stie, p. 90, l. 48, ascend.

Stiȝ, p. 55, l. 460, ascended ; A.S. *stigan*, to ascend, rise.

Stintith, p. 116, l. 62, stoppeth.

Sue, p. 20, l. 68, follow.

Suffraunce, p. 33, l. 50, Fr. *souffrance*, sufferance, forbearance, patience, abiding.

Sunge, p. 110, l. 73, sin ; A.S. *syngian*.

Superflue, p. 89, l. 30, superfluous.

Swarte, p. 119, l. 33, dark, black (swarthy).

Swing, p. 28, l. 203, A.S. *swingan*, to whip, scourge.

Swiþe, p. 69, l. 348, quickly.

Swyde, p. 122, l. 140, quickly.

Swynk, p. 89, l. 32, A.S. *swine*, labour, *yeswine*, affliction, torment.

Temynge, p. 4, l. 20, childbirth; A.S. *team*, offspring; *teámian*, *téman*, to propagate, beget.

Tende, p. 69, l. 369; tenden, p. 41, l. 6, attend.

Tene, p. 24, l. 71, A.S. *teóna*, injury, wrong.

þat þat, p. 51, l. 310, that which.

þee, p. 63, l. 176, thrive.

þertille, p. 9, l. 37, thereto, in addition.

þirle, p. 26, l. 147, pierce; A.S. *þirlian*.

þole, p. 23, l. 27, A.S. *þolian*, suffer.

þrong, p. 13, l. 27, driven, forced; A.S. *þringan*, to press, crowd.

þrouჳ, p. 13, l. 32, A.S. *þruh*, a chest, coffin, sepulchre, grave.

Tille, p. 27, l. 168, to.

Toberste, p. 30, l. 251, burst all to pieces.

Tobreke, p. 29, l. 247, break to pieces.

Torent, p. 20, l. 82, rent to pieces.

Towe, p. 120, l. 29, tough, harsh; A.S. *tóh*.

Towyth, p. 121, l. 108, thought.

Twhertyd, p. 126, l. 15, retorted? A.S. *hweorfan*, to turn.

Twynne, p. 23, l. 37, separate.

Tyne, p. 25, l. 103, A.S. *tynan*, to hedge in, enclose, shut, close.

Vertu, p. 67, l. 300, power, strength.

Vertu, p. 72, l. 455, power, strength.

Vncele, p. 106, l. 21, unhappiness.

Vndirfonge, p. 69, l. 367, receive, take; A.S. *underfangan*, undertake, receive.

Vndirnome, p. 50, l. 289, ? tookest up or under, objectedst to; A.S. *underniman*, to undertake, comprehend.

Vngo, p. 121, l. 118, ? *vn* for *um*, round; A.S. *ymbgan*, go round.

Vndren, p. 84, l. 25, A.S. *undern*, the third hour, 9 a.m., extending also to noon.

Vnleueful, p. 110, l. 74, unlawful.

Vnneþe, p. 70, l. 373, A.S. *unédelice*, uneasily, with difficulty, scarcely, hardly.

Vnourne, p. 71, l. 404, A.S. *vnórnlic*, old, worn.

Vnsauჳte, p. 108, l. 37, unfriendly; A.S. *seht*, friendship, peace; *unseht*, want of friendship, enmity. Note the *unsoft* of the later text, p. 109.

Vnschent, p. 106, l. 6, unpunished.

Vnskilfully, p. 112, l. 90, unreasonably; *see* skil.

Vusperid, p. 41, l. 15, set free, unlocked; 'speryn, or schettyn, *claudo;* speryn and schette wythe lokkys. Sero, obsero.' Pr. Parv.

Waitist, p. 50, l. 288, plannest.

Wake, p. 32, l. 8.; p. 99, l. 141, watch; A.S. *wacan*.

Wan, p. 13, l. 41, wonnst, wentest.

Waterless, p. 20, l. 53, without water.

Wedde, p. 10, l. 60, pledge; A.S. *wed*.

Wede, p. 12, l. 18, garment; A.S. *wéd*.

Welkid, p. 24, l. 68, faded, turned white; A.S. *wealcere*, a fuller, a whitener of cloths.

Wem, p. 83, l. 13, spot, A.S. *wem*.

Wente, p. 9, l. 51, gone.

Were, p. 106, 107, l. 2, danger;

A.S. *wér*, a fine for slaying a man ; p. 116, l. 87, doubt ?

Weuere, p. 77, l. 603, weaver, contriver, schemer.

White, p. 72, l. 450, quick, active ; same as

Wiȝte, p. 63, l. 150 ; Sw. *vig*, active ; '*wyte*, or delyvyr, or swyfte, Agilis, velox.' Pr. Parv.

Wiȝtli, p. 13, l. 41, swiftly, or powerfully.

Wijs, p. 98, l. 94, teach.

Wis, p. 11, l. 115 ; Wisse, p. 14, l. 68; A.S. *wissian*, to instruct, guide, govern.

Wite, p. 34, l. 67 ; p. 99, l. 4, know ; A.S. *witan*.

Wiyte, p. 35, l. 8, 16, &c., blame, reproach, impute, ascribe to ; A.S. *witan, witian*.

Wone, p. 11, l. 120, dwell; A.S. *wunian*.

Woniynge, p. 28, l. 199, dwelling.

Woost, p. 39, l. 35, knowest.

Worschipide, p. 53, l. 401, honoured.

Wreche, p. 16, l. 35, vengeance ; A.S. *wræc*.

Ȝeere, p. 65, l. 214 ; p. 67, l. 286, ? A.S. *geare*, certainly.

Ȝeme, p. 52, l. 340 ; A.S. *gieman*, govern, take care of.

Ȝernynge, p. 28, l. 197, yearning, desire.

Ȝore, p. 92, l. 35, formerly.

Yllet, p. 92, l. 37, fled, gone.

Yhit, p. 128, l. 3, yet.

Yloore, p. 79, l. 5, lost; A.S. *loren*.

Ymet, p. 81, l. 74, dreamt; A.S. *mætod*.

Ynne, p. 69, l. 359, ? bring in, not let in ; A.S. *innan*, to go in, enter.

Ynow, p. 76, l. 567, enough.

NOTES.

P. 58. *Mirror of the Periods of Man's Life.* "The auncient sages by curious notes haue found out, that certaine yeeres in mans life be very perilous. These they name climacterical or stayric yeares, for then they saw great alterations. Now a climactericall yeare is euery seauenth yeare .. Hence is it that in the seauenth yeere children doe cast and renew their teeth. In the fourteenth yeere proceedeth the stripling age. In the one and twentieth, youth. And when a man hath past seauen times seauen years, to weet, nine and fortie yeares, he is a ripe and perfect man. Also, when he attaineth to ten times seauen yeeres, that is, to the age of threescore and ten, his strength and chiefest vertue beginnes to fall away." W. Vaughan, Natural and Artificial Directions for Health, 1602, pp. 47-8.

P. 128. Archbishop Scrope's Death. See the Latin Poem on this in Mr. Thomas Wright's "Political Songs," v. 2, p. 114-18.

INDEX OF FIRST LINES.

	Page
As y gan wandre in my walkinge	83
Bi a forest as y gan walke	95
Bothe ȝonge & oolde, wheþir ȝe be	32
Erþe out of erþe is wondirly wrouȝt	88
Euery man schulde teche þis lore	104
From þe tyme þat we were born	79
Hay, hay, hay, hay! thynke on Whitsonmonday	128
Heil be þou, marie, cristis moder dere	6
Heil be þou, marie, þe modir of crist	4
How mankinde dooþ bigynne. (The Mirror.)	58
If þou wole be weel with god. (A prose piece.)	40
Ihesu, lord, þat madist me. (Richard de Castre's Prayer.)	15
Ihesu, þi swetnes, who-so myȝte it se	8
Ihesus þat sprong of iesse roote	12
In a noon tijd of a somers day	91
In my ȝonge age ful wielde y was	35
In þee, god fadir, I bileeue	101
I warne vche leod þat liueþ in londe (From the Vernon MS.)	106
I warne eche lijf þat liueþ in lond	107

Page

Kyng of grace, & ful of pyte . . . 118

Loue is lijf þat lastiþ ay . . . 22

Man, among þi myrþis haue in mynde 114

Sodenly a-frayd, halfe wakynge, halfe slepyng . . 126
Surge, mea sponsa, swete in siȝt . . 1

There is no creature but oon 18

Whanne marye was greet with gabriel. (þe Deuelis Perlament) 41
Whi is þis world biloued þat fals is & veyn . . . 86

JOHN CHILDS AND SON, PRINTERS.

www.ingramcontent.com/pod-product-compliance
Lightning Source LLC
Chambersburg PA
CBHW021124020726
47500CB00003B/907